Praise for *T...*

With a soulful intensity, Grant succe...
to freedom and in challenging wom...
joyously, unfettered by society's unre...

Christian women spend a great deal of time discussing how "the world" negatively impacts the way we see and value ourselves. We are pros in discussing the epidemic of plastic surgery, the frightening trend in extreme dieting, and the alarming increase of women with eating disorders. This is how our culture chases beauty and perfection. And we speak about these issues with the naive and smug assumption that they would never . . . *could* never . . . find their way into our Bible believing, Christian homes. This is why Natalie Grant deserves a giant high five from a lot of us. In *The Real Me*, she basically takes a deep breath and tells the hard truth, shining the light on some very real and very dark ways that we believe lie upon lie about what makes us beautiful . . . and the countless ways we sabotage our roles as precious daughters of God. And get this: she was raised in a Christian home with all the blessings of a strong foundation . . . and she was still a fair target. Can I get an amen? You will find yourself nodding repeatedly as you identify with so many of her brave admissions. Ideally, this book should be read by every teenage girl who's ever stood too long in front of a mirror and wished for something much more than God, who with great care and purpose, granted her. And then, even more ideally, each of those girls should hand the book to her mother. Bravo, Natalie. And thank you.

—Nichole Nordeman
Dove Award Winning Singer/Songwriter, *Brave*

In this compelling and captivating story, Natalie Grant unfolds her personal struggle with self-image issues, which eventually led to bulimia. Natalie's honesty and transparency is sure to connect with the heart of any girl, regardless of her age. I commend Natalie for having the courage to boldly share what will undoubtedly set countless girls on the path to freedom.

—Nancy Alcorn
President and Founder, Mercy Ministries

This book is like a song that pierces your soul. So real. Surprisingly honest. Natalie has the guts to say what so many only dare to think and feel. Every girl will find herself somewhere in the pages of this book and then . . . begin to see the girl God sees and get real.

—Lisa Ryan
Feature Host, *700 Club*

I am moved by Natalie's honesty and poignancy. This book will speak volumes to both the secure and those that think they're secure. Great job Natalie!

—Lisa Kimmey
Dove Award Winning Artist/Songwriter/Producer

In *The Real Me*, Natalie Grant exposes her struggles in a desire to help encourage teens in a society pressured by perfection. As a teen, I desperately relate to her insecurities and battles with self image in the war to be genuinely confident in the girl I'm created to be.

—Joy Ladd
Co-author, *The Power of a Positive Teen*

Natalie related to so many of the feelings I have had and continue to have as a teen girl and as someone in the media. After reading *The Real Me* I felt like someone finally understood what it was like to be tested, not only in my faith in God, but in what I think about myself, how I push myself for acceptance. Natalie, thank you for sharing your story and for caring about the struggles of self-image in girls. God Bless!

—Austin-Nichole Zachrich
Host/Creator, Austin-Nichole & Co. Teen Television Program

In *The Real Me*, Natalie Grant not only referred to her own life struggles and situations, but she used other people's unique stories so that anyone could find themselves in this book. Personally I don't understand what it's like to have an eating disorder, but there are other places in my life that I could compare the principles to. The words that God used through her were good and helped me a lot.

—Allie
16 years old

A truly inspirational book, Natalie helps girls understand how God sees them and how to view themselves through God's lens and not the worlds. Both encouraging and motivating, *The Real Me* inspires females to overcome the lies the world is constantly feeding them—images of unrealistic beauty, ridiculous expectations, and false hope.

—Tamara
19 years old

The Real Me is the song of Natalie Grant's heart. On each page she sings to us of her most precious lesson, how she learned to live in God's love. Hers is a melody we all long to sing: we are loved. Indeed, we are loved.

—Nika
29 years old

the REAL ME

the REAL ME

Being the Girl God Sees

Natalie Grant

THOMAS NELSON
Since 1798

NASHVILLE DALLAS MEXICO CITY RIO DE JANEIRO BEIJING

Published in Nashville, Tennessee by Thomas Nelson. Thomas Nelson is a trademark of Thomas Nelson, Inc.

Thomas Nelson Inc. titles may be purchased in bulk for educational, business, fundraising, or sales promotional use. For information, please e-mail SpecialMarkets@ThomasNelson.com.

Unless otherwise indicated, all Scripture quotations are taken from The Holy Bible, New Century Version, copyright © 1987, 1988, 1991 by Word Publishing, Dallas, Texas 75234. Used by permission. Other Scripture passages are from the following versions: The King James Version (KJV). THE HOLY BIBLE, NEW INTERNATIONAL VERSION® (NIV). Copyright © 1973, 1978, 1984 International Bible Society. Used by permission of Zondervan. All rights reserved. *The Message* (MSG), copyright © 1993, 1994, 1995, 1996, 2000, 2001, 2002. Used by permission of NavPress Publishing Group. The New King James Version (NKJV). Copyright © 1982 by Thomas Nelson, Inc. Used by permission. All rights reserved. The Holy Bible, New Living Translation (NLV), copyright © 1996. Used by permission of Tyndale House Publishers, Inc., Wheaton, Illinois 60189. All rights reserved.

Personal profiles in this volume are true; however, in some instances names and details have been changed to protect identities. Appreciation goes to each individual whose profile has been used with permission.

Portions of lyrics reprinted throughout this volume are taken from the song "The Real Me," Natalie Grant, © 2004 Nat·In·The·Hat Music. Admin. by The Loving Company. All Rights Reserved. Used By Permission.

Library of Congress Cataloging-in-Publication Data

Grant, Natalie, 1971–
  The real me : being the girl God sees / by Natalie Grant.
    p. cm.
  Summary: "Contemporary Christian singer/songwriter Natalie Grant offers help and hope for women struggling with the issues of self-image"—Provided by publisher.
  Includes bibliographical references.
  ISBN 10: 0-8499-0882-5 (tradepaper)
  ISBN 13: 978-0-8499-0882-8 (tradepaper)
  1. Self-perception—Religious aspects—Christianity. 2. Christian women—Religious life. I. Title.
  BV4598.25.G73 2005
  248.8'43—dc22   2005015537

Printed in the United States of America
07 08 09 10 11 RRD 9 8 7 6 5 4

For Jenna and Savannah

Contents

Acknowledgments

This book is my story. However, I cannot accept all the credit for getting it onto these pages. So many wonderful and talented people helped me on this journey, and I would not have been able to add "author" to my resume without them.

First, I give honor to Jesus, the true Author of my life. I am so grateful to be a child of God.

Debbie Wickwire: you are a gem! Thank you for believing in my ability to write this book. I said, "I cannot." But you said, "Yes, you can." Thank you for your faith in me.

David Moberg, Debbie Nichols, Renee Reed, Karen Phillips, Mary Hollingsworth, Lori Lynch, Jeff Loper, Heather Adams, Caroline Craddock, and the entire staff at Thomas Nelson: what an honor to work with all of you. Without you, this book would still be a figment of my imagination.

Melissa Riddle: you have partnered with me in this project every step of the way. Thank you for your additions. Your words paint such beautiful pictures.

Mary Graham and the staff of Women of Faith, Girls of

Faith, and the Revolve Tour: you have given me such an incredible platform. I am honored to be a part of your family.

Christie Barnes: you are a good friend who always believed I could accomplish this. Thank you!

Sue Ann Jones: you are the icing on the cake. Your touch is just what I needed to make it complete.

Mom and Dad: thank you for your enormous amount of love and support. Most of all, thank you for showing me Jesus.

Beth, Allison, Steve, and Jennifer: I am so glad I am your "lil" sis! Thanks for your constant love and belief in me, and your interest in what I am doing.

And to my husband, Bernie: you are my sounding board, my dictionary, my thesaurus, my cheerleader, and my best friend. Thank you for not judging me, thank you for accepting me, and thank you for loving me.

Fresh from the Fall

Ames, Iowa
Winter 2003

*M*y curtain call was quickly approaching. I was on tour with several different bands, and as the only female, I had a dressing room completely to myself. I wanted to look my best that night, so I had spent a little extra time getting ready, pulling on the cutest pair of jeans, tall stiletto boots, and a sassy black leather hat. Right before I headed out the door, I prayed the prayer I always pray before facing the stage lights: "Lord, be glorified through my music, and may the words of my mouth and the meditation of my heart please you."

1

My band members took their respective places, then I waltzed into the spotlight, smiling my brightest smile and eager to get started. It was going to be a good night. I could feel it.

As we started the first song, I could hear the enthusiastic roar of the five thousand people in the audience. Each face seemed to be filled with warm encouragement, and the crowd's expectant energy filled the auditorium. The groove my band was laying down felt great, and I was belting out "Keep on Shining" at the top of my lungs.

Then I fell off the stage.

Yes, you read that correctly. *I fell off the stage!* I don't know exactly what went wrong. I had done that set of music many times before and always managed to stay on my feet, but somehow, this time was different. I'd like to blame the incident on one of the floor monitors—a speaker that plays back the sound of the band and my voice so I can hear what's happening. But the truth is, those monitors were in the same spot on the stage they always were, and the one I tripped over certainly didn't jump out in front of me. But for some reason, on the last note of my first song, I walked right into it, lost my balance, flipped through an aerial movement that surely would have scored at least an 8.0 in any Olympic competition, and tumbled off the stage into the crowd.

At least part of me landed in the crowd; the other part was still dangling from the stage.

Fortunately (at least for me—the folks I fell on might not have felt so fortunate), people were standing right up against the platform, and they caught me. Otherwise I would have fallen right on my head. If I had been thinking, I could have pretended to crowd-surf, although I've never been one for mosh pits. (OK, I've moshed in my mind many times but have never been quite cool enough to act it out.)

I guess the production crew had never seen an artist take a dive off the stage before, because none of them seemed to have a clue what to do. Finally the lighting engineer turned off the stage lights, probably hoping to diminish the sight of me sprawled between the edge of the stage and my human safety net. Thoughtfully, those kind people pushed me back up on the stage, where I lay for moment curled up in the fetal position, probably thinking, *Lord, is there any chance you misunderstood when I asked that you would be* glorified *through my performance tonight? Maybe you thought I said* horrified?

I had been using a corded microphone, and as I went down, the mike went hurling into the crowd. Still lying on the stage but now hunched up like an armadillo, I pulled on the cord, yanking it in like a fishing line caught on a rock. Then I just lay there on the stage another moment, lost in the darkness, ready to burst into both tears and laughter at the same time.

Girl, you've got two choices, I told myself: *get off the stage while it's still dark and never show your face in Ames, Iowa, again, or get up and keep going.*

I got up.

I had injured my ankle in the fall, but the real injury was to my pride. Although I was embarrassed, humiliated, insecure, and unsure of myself, I finished my show. Some of the other artists on the tour helped me up onto a stool. My injured ankle made it difficult to stand, so I took off my stiletto boots and finished the rest of my set in my socks. I was just thankful they were clean. Then I looked down and saw my pinkie toe peeking out of a small hole . . .

THE NEW NATALIE

I have not always been strong enough to make a fool of myself in front of thousands of people then blink back tears, regain my composure, share a laugh, and carry on with the show. The old Natalie would have run off that stage (OK, maybe limped off the stage, given the bad ankle) and rushed straight into a bathroom stall.

Then I might have forced myself to vomit. I know such behavior doesn't make sense to most people, but in some twisted way, that forced purging used to help the old Natalie regain some sense of control.

But that was then. That was before I realized what a powerful influence self-image can be—for bad or for good.

The old Natalie's self-image was one of deception, shame, and failure. But as the new Natalie, I'm learning what it means to be real. I'm working each day to recognize and appreciate the unique person God created me to be. And I'm learning to see that person, that Natalie, through God's eyes. The difference has been life changing.

I mean, I always believed in God and could cite chapter and verse proving that he created me in his image. But somehow I didn't live out the truth of those Scripture passages. It was as if that person God created in his own image was some other Natalie, not me.

When I began to understand that God sees the real me and believes in me, even when I make mistakes, I finally understood that he doesn't expect me to be perfect. That understanding didn't happen overnight. It has been a continual, ongoing, daily process. And let's be honest: it's been work. But the results have been well worth the effort.

This book is my invitation to you to join me in the process of discovering and accepting our true self. In the process, I hope you'll experience the same marvelous, extraordinary change I've felt as I've become the girl God sees.

All Part of His Plan

In the following pages you will learn just how weak I have been in my life. I still have moments when the old

Natalie threatens to move back in and allow the opinions of others to dictate my self-worth. Even now, I still care very much about what others think of me, and my self-esteem is still quite fragile. But I try to be *most* concerned, not about what others think of me, but about an audience of One. God is my primary audience. He's the One whose opinion matters most to me. And even when things go wrong and I end up feeling foolish in front of a crowd, I know God has given me a purpose—something to do that pleases him and carries his message—and I simply try my best to do it.

When I fell off the stage that night in Ames, I was embarrassed, to say the least. In fact, *mortified* was more like it! But by the time I was back on my feet, I knew God wanted to use even that clumsy moment, along with the gift of music he's given me, to encourage the people at the concert. I'm well aware that God has a long-standing record of taking the least likely, the losers, the miserable misfits, and transforming them into leaders of the faith. So, once I was able to uncurl from the fetal position, I knew he would use my most embarrassing moment as part of his plan. God wanted me to be vulnerable, and he also wanted people to see that when things don't go our way, we don't have to run and hide. With his help, we get up and face the situation head-on.

Seeking Release from an Emotional Prison

I have yet to meet one person who has not struggled with his or her self-esteem at some point in life. However, we all struggle to different degrees and handle our insecurities in widely ranging ways. I handled mine the only way I knew how: with a damaging eating disorder. Many of you struggle daily in that same prison, fighting that same psychological disease.

Others of you are coping with insecurities, fears, and lack of self-worth by experimenting with drugs and alcohol. You may think you're the life of the party, but the truth is that your life is now or soon will be out of control. Some of you are medicating your pain with sexual promiscuity, seeking love, affection, and acceptance wherever you can find it. You may even be dealing with your problems by cutting yourself because you are full of so much depression, anger, sadness, and rage that slicing your flesh brings you a strange release and a sense of control. Still others of you may not be "acting out" at all, but on the inside, you constantly rip away at your self-image, inflicting horrible emotional wounds on yourself with words sharper than any blade.

If you're coping with whatever is going on in your head by using one of these (or other) dysfunctional and dangerous methods, you feel tossed out—discarded and rejected. You are ashamed, and you feel alone. Shipwrecked on a deserted island with no rescue in sight.

I know that island well: been there, done that, wrote the tour guide.

It would have been easy to find myself back on that island as I lay on the stage in Ames. I was in a room with five thousand people, yet the old Natalie would have felt all alone lying there in that most unflattering of positions, horrified and humiliated. But the real me knew that God was right beside me on that stage. The new Natalie remembered that I'm never an embarrassment to him. No matter what I do, I belong to him; I'm always accepted.

I know lots of people were laughing at me that night. But instead of allowing their response to throw me into a tailspin, I laughed too. I got up, I laughed, and I carried on. Yes, I had wiped out. But success is not about how you start; it's about how you finish. This journey through life can be hard and get really messy at times. We're bound to fall down. But each time we get up again we learn another valuable lesson.

This book is my story, a journey through the lessons I've learned as I've struggled to regain my self-worth when life has knocked me down. Maybe you will see some of your own story in mine; if so, I pray that my experiences help you see that you are not alone in your struggles.

Please remember that your questions are not too big for God, and your pain does not go unnoticed. Take the Scripture lessons in this book to heart, learn from my mistakes and my victories, and seek out the peace and sense of value God wants for his children. I encourage you to journal the journey, and I've left spaces to write down your thoughts as we move through these pages together. I hope, by the time you've come to the end of the book, you can look back and trace the path that has led you to become the girl God sees.

chapter one

Divine Awakening

> *Foolish heart,*
> *Looks like we're here again.*
> *Same old game of plastic smile—*
> *Don't let anybody in.*

Something was wrong. This had never happened before. I was completely repulsed by the smell. Typically, throwing up was exhilarating. Purging was a natural high. Whenever I did it, I felt in control. But today was different. Why?

I had gone through my normal routine: *Make sure no one in my family is anywhere near the bathroom—check. Faucet turned on to hide the retching noise—check. Toilet paper tucked around the collar of my shirt and sleeves to avoid the splash—check.* With everything taken care of, I began the process of becoming "clean" again.

I must get rid of the food. ALL of it.

If you've never struggled with an eating disorder, this probably sounds totally bizarre to you. On the other hand, if you're locked in a several-times-a-day purging ritual, as I was, it all sounds painfully familiar, doesn't it?

As strange as it is, I actually enjoyed heaving, that gagging reflex that came right before I regurgitated. I don't know why I liked it so much. There is nothing pleasant about vomiting; still, the feeling was strangely comforting. I would usually gag a few times before the food came up. And knowing that once would never fully do the trick, I would put my finger down my throat for a second round and a third and so on until I felt completely emptied out. I was always fearful that I might not get rid of everything I had eaten.

But this time, after just one heave, I was disgusted by the stench and the appearance of my vomit. Normally (like there's anything *normal* about this behavior), I would close my eyes, thinking that if I couldn't see it, it was somehow less real. Maybe I was trying to pretend someone else was retching into the commode, not me. But on that day, I was so repelled by the pungent smell, I opened my eyes and stared into the toilet.

Suddenly I felt as though a huge spotlight had focused right on me, and I was seeing myself as an outsider would.

How did I get here? my mind seemed to ask. *How could I end up like this, hovering over the toilet, knees numb to the pain of kneeling on a cold, hard tile floor?*

The shame and humiliation I felt in that moment rose up from my heart into my throat, imagining what others would think if they could see me now. I'd always tried so hard to be the perfect girl. The life of the party. The leader. The person everyone else came to with his or her problems.

But I had a problem too, a huge, painful secret, and I couldn't hide it—or hide from it—any longer.

Vogue on the Outside, Vague on the Inside

I wish I could tell you in vivid detail what snapped in me that day. But to be perfectly honest, I don't know. It was a typical day. By all outward appearances, I was a happy, well-adjusted overachiever. But bulimia had become a way of life for me. I had become the queen of disguise, so much so that I had begun believing my own act.

What I called my "churchianity" was better than ever, Oscar-worthy, even. I could quote lots of Scripture verses to prove my Christian maturity. Everyone thought I was so spiritual, so perfect; but I wasn't. Somehow the twelve-inch span from my head to my heart had become the Grand Canyon, and there seemed to be no way to bridge the gap. I felt lost. I had been so busy being who everyone thought I was that I no longer had a sense of being real. And because I knew I was being dishonest, living a lie, I felt worthless.

Everyone thought I was so brave, but I wasn't. I believed that if my family and friends knew the real me, they would be ashamed. They would despise me.

The truth was, I despised myself.

I desperately wanted to be accepted. I cared so intensely about what other people thought of me that pleasing everyone became my focal point, the driving force behind everything I did. The pressure was overwhelming and constant. Totally vogue on the outside but completely vague on the inside: that was me.

Having successfully fooled everyone around me into believing my mythical life of perfection, I never considered the cost of maintaining the charade.

Now, don't get me wrong. I knew Jesus loved me, and I believed it wholeheartedly. At least I thought I did.

I didn't suffer from the Jesus-could-never-love-somebody-as-pitiful-as-me syndrome. At least I thought I didn't.

Jesus became my Savior when I was a little girl, but I don't think I ever allowed him to become my Lord. A lord is the master, someone who has complete power, control, and authority.

Problem was, *I* was the lord of my life.

REAL GIRL, REAL LIFE

The Weight of Perfection

There are always people we secretly wish we could be or at least be like. We're certain our life would be better if we had their, well, fill in the blank: _____.

Jessica is one of those girls, the kind of striking stand-out who not only seems to have it all but also has it all together. She's a blonde, blue-eyed beauty, five feet six inches tall, who wears a size 2 and is superintelligent and artistically talented. She is also one of the leaders in her high school and has two wonderful parents and a sister who love her dearly.

So she's living happily ever after, right?

Sure she is—until you look deeper.

Although Jessica would probably admit that she's generally a happy person who is truly grateful for the blessings in her life, when asked what has been the hardest thing about being a teenage girl she doesn't hesitate a second.

"The weight issue," she replies. "This year has changed so much for me. I don't know if it's because I've got more responsibility, but I've just started to worry about things more—especially my weight. I don't skip meals too frequently, but sometimes I do because I'm so busy. I never look at calories, but there've been a couple of times when I've just eaten something and felt disgusting. And then I've thrown it up."

Her mother doesn't believe in having scales in the house, but Jessica still manages to keep a close eye on her weight by weighing herself at other homes during her frequent babysitting jobs. She says her concern about her weight, her body, and what she's eating is a continual source of noise in her head, which, she admits, is probably why she's made herself throw up.

But are her issues with food rooted completely in wanting to look a certain way?

"I don't feel like I'm overweight by a lot," she confesses, "but I feel like I could lose some weight. I guess if I had the right mind-set I wouldn't worry about the way I look. Part of it isn't even a weight issue. Sometimes I feel so frustrated and overwhelmed with stuff that the eating part of my life is the only thing I can grasp and control. Take grades, for instance. I can study really hard and not make a good grade, and I can't control that. Sometimes [monitoring my weight] feels like making sure that I have control of myself and my life."

WHO'S IT GONNA BE? YOU OR ME?

That day in the bathroom, a divine intervention began for me in the unlikeliest of places—as I lay curled around the base of the toilet. Suddenly I knew for certain I could no longer continue to live the way I was living. Bulimia was not the abundant life God intended me to live. I finally understood that I was trapped in a prison of my own making, and I knew Jesus was the only One who could set me free.

As I picked myself up off the floor, I remembered that God had promised he would make "all things work together for good" (Romans 8:28 NKJV), but I couldn't imagine what purpose he could create out of my pain. I was weak and confused, but hope had awakened inside me, and I wasn't turning back. That day, on the hard, cold floor, God made me wonderfully uncomfortable, beautifully tortured by the chaos of my condition. I had no idea who I was anymore, but on that day, with God's help, I set out in search of the real me.

> *But you see the real me*
> *Hiding in my skin*
> *Broken from within.*

The Real You

Is there a secret in your life, something you've held on to for a long time, hoping nobody sees it? Something so painful, so far down in your heart, that you dare not even speak of it? If so, there's something you should know: you're not alone. I know you might not believe it now, but maybe soon you will. In the meantime, can you muster up enough courage to personalize those words and write "I'M NOT ALONE" in the space below?

Are You Ready for a Divine Awakening?

My poor self-esteem reared its ugly head as an eating disorder. What consequences are *you* struggling with as a result of a poor self-image? Do you have secrets that make you feel worthless? In your effort to exert control, are you inflicting damage on yourself physically or emotionally? If so, you're probably overdue for a moment of divine intervention. Please open your heart and your mind to God's presence and pray this prayer: "God, wake up my mind to the truth of who I am, who you created me to be, and to the truth of who you are. Gather the feelings and emotions in my head and give me the courage to be honest about myself. And most of all, give me faith to believe what you have to teach

God says, "Let Me . . ."

Anyone who intends to come with me has to let me lead. You're not in the driver's seat; I am. Don't run from suffering; embrace it. Follow me and I'll show you how. Self-help is no help at all. Self-sacrifice is the way, my way, to finding yourself, you're true self. What kind of deal is it to get everything you want but lose yourself? (Matthew 16:24–26 MSG)

me as I study your Word and read Natalie's book. I want a divine awakening, Lord. I need to know you're here with me. Amen."

Be receptive to God's love for you, his gift of peace—watch for it, expect it—even in the unlikeliest places. He surrounded me with his comforting love and acceptance as I lay curled around the toilet on the floor of a bathroom. Where will *you* be when you finally give in to his extraordinary, healing grace?

Just Like You: Young Women Who Touched the World

Amelia Earhart: Courage Is the Price

When twenty-year-old Amelia Earhart attended a stunt-flying exhibition, a plane swooped overhead, and she was enthralled. "I did not understand it at the time," she said later, "but I believe that little red airplane said something to me as it swished by."

In December 1920, when she experienced her first airplane ride, Amelia knew she had to fly. Becoming an aviator was no easy feat for a woman during that era, but Amelia was no stranger to obstacles. She was the child of an alcoholic whose drinking often cost him his job, so Amelia and her family moved around a lot, and Amelia and her sister attended many different schools. Still, Amelia worked hard and excelled academically, and that determination helped her become a successful aviator.

By 1921, Amelia Earhart had saved up enough money to take flying lessons, and soon after she learned to fly she bought her own plane, which she called The Canary. In that plane she set a women's flying record by soaring to an altitude of fourteen thousand feet. She continued to set records throughout the rest of her aviation career and became a celebrity for being the first woman to fly across the Atlantic Ocean in 1928. Although she presumably died (her body was never found) while trying to fly around the world in 1937, her feats are still celebrated as a part of American history.

It was the courage of Amelia Earhart that endeared her to so many. From the time she was a young girl, she took risks despite being afraid. She lived in a world where women often were told no when they wanted to try the things men could do. To this response—and to all of us today—she said, "Women must try to do things as men have tried. When they fail, their failure must be but a challenge to others."

Now thousands of women, following in the footsteps of this tomboy who was determined to fly, sit in the cockpits of commercial, military, and privately owned aircraft all over the world. Like Amelia Earhart, they have chosen to face their fears and take the risks necessary to achieve their goals, and today they are a living legacy of the woman who listened to her heart and said, "Courage is the price that life exacts for granting peace."

Picture-Perfect

Hiding my heartache,
Will this glass house break?
How much will they take before I'm empty?
Do I let it show?
Does anybody know?

My childhood was almost picture-perfect. My parents were (and still are) happily married. My dad always worked very hard to make sure our life was comfortable. Mom stayed home and was the happy homemaker. We were the family who ate every dinner around the table together, and it was our most cherished time of the day. We genuinely loved being together.

So how did I get from such a loving, carefree existence—where the calluses on my hands came only from twirling around a bar on the playground—to calluses on my hands from sitting on that cold, hard bathroom floor forcing myself to vomit? How did I get from a supportive, nurturing home life to a mental state where I felt emptied of all emotional nourishment and full of self-loathing? Where did that self-destructive behavior coming from?

For the answer, I had to dive in and swim to the deep recesses of my heart.

A House Full of Love

I was born and raised in Seattle, the city that gave us Starbucks and Microsoft. Progressive, artsy . . . there's no place like it in the world. I am so intrigued by the city, so smitten by her grandeur. There is such beauty revealed in her statuesque trees, majestic towering mountains, and the mystery of foggy mornings.

Everything I wish I could be and all the things I am not . . .

For starters, what I am is short, or maybe the politically correct term is *petite*. I'm five feet four on a good day, but because my legs are so short, most people guess I'm really about five one or five two. Actually, there *was* a time when I was tall. So what if it was in the fifth grade? I got to stand on the back row for the classroom picture, which, as I look back on it now, was my last memorable event as a tall person.

It didn't feel so great *then* to be tall, however. I was

eleven years old, and I was having a tough year. I didn't want to be the first girl in my class to wear a bra or the first to experience a bad mood followed by a maxi pad—which is exactly what happened, and of course it was just in time to keep me out of the pool at my friend's swimming party. Life is so cruel!

To make matters worse, I had just had my hair permed. Now, maybe permed hair doesn't sound very traumatic, but when it's permed by your sweet older sister Allison, who is "just trying to save the family money," *traumatic* is the understatement of the year!

Fifth grade is tough enough, but add in my sudden "growth spurt of the chest" and the bunch of cauliflower on my head otherwise known as my hair (the perm truly was awful), and needless to say, I went through an uncharacteristically introverted phase.

But other than those temporary horrors that made me want to crawl under a rock, I lived my life out loud. From the time I was a little girl, I was always the center of attention—the apple of my daddy's eye, my mommy's little princess, and my siblings' favorite toy. Even back then, I recognized what a privilege it was to be raised in a house full of love. I knew with certainty that I was loved, and I knew that being born into the Grant family was a gift. No family is perfect, but I honestly thought mine was.

That sweet misconception is where the pressure for perfection was born inside me.

We all have them, those dreaded school pictures. The heart-achingly awful ones taken every year, the little portraits that live in infamy for years to come in the pages of school yearbooks and on the walls in our houses. They are testimonies to every bad-hair day, every telltale sign of imperfection experienced throughout our most awkward years. At best, they help us remember who we were once upon a time. At worst, they remind us of all we are not, all we wish we could be.

In the space below, write about either your best-ever or your worst-ever school picture. (If you're like me, you'll have a hard time deciding which one is truly the worst!) Tell why you think it's so bad. Be honest. Then, when you're finished, complete this sentence: "But underneath what can be seen, I was/am a girl who . . ."

If I could take you through the photo album of my life, on page after page, picture after picture, you would see a free-spirited, energetic girl who always found her way to the center of the photograph. In every frame and with every pose, you would sense my zest for life. And you would see a natural leader, a take-charge kind of girl. OK, maybe just a little bit bossy at times too.

It all made sense. After all, I came from a long line of winners. I was the youngest, the adorable baby, the pride and joy of a solid family with an impeccable heritage. That was the gift I'd been given.

It was also the curse I imagined: the reputation I felt I could never quite live up to.

My family members' giant footsteps loomed so large in my mind, they seemed impossible for me to follow:

My oldest sister, Bethenee, was president of her class and a true scholar.

My sister Allison had the quiet confidence, the perfect hair, and the perfect boyfriend, who eventually became the perfect husband. (She did have one flaw: she gave terrible perms!)

My brother, Steve, was an A across the board: academic, athletic, artistic, and amazing at everything. He was a success at whatever he did.

Last but not least, my sister Jennifer was and is beautiful and popular, sweet and endearing. Every girl wanted to be her, and every boy wanted to date her.

I reviewed the trail of accomplishments my siblings had blazed and thought, *What if I'm the first underachiever in the Grant family?* Then I looked around and remembered that everyone liked me. *I'm special,* I told myself.

At least I'd better be . . .

More Than Just a Pretty Face

Look closely, and you'll see a few silver-gray streaks adorning her bright blue eyes; it's almost as though they're offering a silent clue that Alicia is an artist. In many ways she is a typical seventeen-year-old wrestling with some of the same things most teen girls do. But in one significant way, Alicia has walked a much different path than her friends.

She was born with a benign tumor on her face that has required five surgeries.

"Though I had the tumor all my life," she remembers, "I didn't really get any teasing about it until I moved to Florida in the fourth grade. There was one little boy at my school who was really vindictive. To me, the tumor wasn't really noticeable, but apparently he and a few other people thought it was. It kind of looked like someone had punched me in the lower lip."

It gradually became apparent that her tumor, caused by a condition called lymphangioma, could cause some complications down the road. At age eleven she had surgery to remove it, and she has additional operations since then in an attempt to minimize the scar.

"In the beginning, right after my surgery, it was hard to come to terms with the scar because it was a matter of going from looking one way to looking another," Alicia explains. "But it wasn't long before I didn't think about it too much because I had really cool, accepting friends."

Unfortunately, middle school classmates weren't quite as accepting. It was a season she remembers as hammering away at her self-esteem.

"When I first went into middle school, I think the scar was kind of a shock to some," she reflects. "When it came to talking to random people, I could do that. But when I was talking to a boy I liked, I would sort of panic, thinking, *He can see my scar!* That's bad enough, but throw in puberty and pimples, and it all makes you want to scream. It's overload!"

These days Alicia has traded thoughts about puberty and pimples for dreams about college and her future. And while she hopes to someday be scar-free, she has learned to accept who she is by focusing on what she has instead of what she doesn't have; she takes great pleasure in her artistic gifts.

"I would like to be famous someday with my artwork," she says, "and I find that my emotions, both positive and negative, are powerful inspiration for my drawings."

Contrary to the common portrayal of an attention-starved girl who yearns for the approval and affection of her distant, cold parents, I was blessed with a mom and dad who were there for me every step of the way. Encouraging and loving, they always told me there was no limit to what I could achieve. I was the object of their hopes, maybe even the promise of fulfillment for some of their own unrealized dreams. Yet this relentless, if not maddening, optimism that insisted I was destined for greatness also presented the opportunity for failure.

Failure? No way! I couldn't let them down.

Although we all need affirmation, I may have received it in excess. It was no one's fault but my own, but I guess all the constant praise made me feel like I had to continue doing better and better things to receive it. Maybe my family became too wonderful in my mind, if that's possible, because I adored them so much I was always afraid I might disappoint them.

With that kind of attitude, I became a determined people pleaser. The result was that I grew up seeking my identity in the approval of others. Affirmation became addictive to me, and my hunger for approval found its way into every relationship in my life.

At a very young age, I began receiving a lot of praise for

my singing ability, and I was frequently onstage. I'm sure that constantly being in the spotlight intensified the pressure I felt to please and to meet expectations. Because I never wanted anyone to see my insecurities, I overcompensated for my feelings of inadequacy by oozing confidence.

Sometimes, however, my confident facade was misunderstood or misinterpreted, and criticism or snide remarks came my way. But instead of letting anyone see that I was hurt, broken, and scared, I decided I would be pretty enough, I would be smart enough, and I would be talented enough to rise above the critics.

From this launchpad of conflicting emotions, I headed into my teenage years, a mask of strength firmly in place so my weaknesses wouldn't show.

Instead of being real, I became real successful at wearing that mask. Inside, insecurity scratched at my soul, and at times it felt as if I were two different people. The confident me said, *I'm popular. I'm a cheerleader. People like me. I'm a talented singer, and I will use my gift to cement my place as the star*

The LORD says, "My thoughts are not like your thoughts. Your ways are not like my ways. Just as the heavens are higher than the earth, so are my ways higher than your thoughts." (Isaiah 55:8–9)

of the show. But the overpowering, insecure me whispered, *Remember that moment someone snickered at you in the hall and said you looked fat in your cheerleading uniform?*

Dwelling on that moment, recalling the exact time and place when I overheard the remark, completely deflated me and left me feeling worthless again. But then the mask would slide back into place, and I would hold my head high, proving how tough I was. *Those silly comments can't put a ding in my confident armor.*

But I was *not* tough, and although my mask was set firmly in place, on the inside I was feeling quite crumbly. Then I would remind myself, *I'm Natalie Grant! I may be crumbling, but I can't fall apart. Not me. I have it all together; my life's picture-perfect.*

And then the real Natalie would think, *Or so I've led everyone to believe . . .*

Slowly but surely, my quest for perfection turned its most destructive eye to my outward appearance. I didn't just wake up one day and say, "I want to be skinny. Maybe I'll throw up."

No, the road that led me to that cold, hard bathroom floor was built on my own misconceptions and paved with imaginary pressures that had slowly germinated in my mind. The mask I was wearing had become such a part of my life that I sometimes wondered what would be left of me if it was removed. I was striving to be a perfect people pleaser because I believed that doing for others and living up to others' standards was necessary to be accepted. In my heart I knew I was a failure at attaining perfection, but I didn't realize how severely my misguided quest had damaged my self-worth.

Nobody knew what a big mess I was on the inside. Not even me.

High school graduation neared, and everything seemed to be falling into place perfectly. I was a strong leader in my youth group, my parents were as proud as ever, and I had received a music scholarship to college for my vocal talent. I was an oh-so-big fish in a small pond, and I knew I was the envy of many. I'm sure people looked at my "perfect" life and thought, *That girl has everything going for her.*

Yet I was miserable. I thought, *Why do I give such great advice, yet have no answers for myself? Why, when the lights are out and I'm alone with my thoughts, is the silence my great accuser? I feel such guilt. I am a fraud.*

GETTING REAL WITH GOD: JUST AS I AM

Taking Off the Mask and Getting Real

Chances are, you've sung the old hymn "Just As I Am." I certainly have. In fact, I grew up attending churches that didn't seem to know any other invitation hymn existed. And to be honest, by the time I was eight years old, I didn't like that hymn one bit. I didn't understand all the thees and thous, but it was more than that. I knew I couldn't sing that hymn honestly because I wasn't coming to God "just as I am," and I didn't plan on coming clean with him anytime soon.

Even then, I knew I had too much to hide.

The older I got, the better I became at hiding the real me. In fact, I became a world-class fake. On the outside I was a good Christian girl who "had it all together." I was an impressive youth leader who said all the right things. I had lots of friends and wore all the right clothes. Everyone else bought into my disguise, but I couldn't fool God. It was silly even to try. He already knew my heart completely.

What did it take to set me free? It took the courage to take off my mask. To come out of hiding.

I love the way Brennan Manning describes it in his book *Posers, Fakers, and Wannabes: Unmasking the Real You*:

> No amount of spiritual cosmetology can make us more presentable to God. God buys us in an as-is condition and says, "I've been looking for you! I have just the place for you!"
>
> God, who spoke us into existence, speaks to us now: "Come out of self-hatred into my love. Come to me now," he says. "Forget about yourself. Accept who I long to be for you, who I am for you—your Rescuer—endlessly loving, forever patient, unbearably forgiving. . . .

You are a broken flower—I will not crush you—a flickering candle, I will not extinguish you. For once and forever, relax: of all places, *you are safe with me.*"[1]

What an amazing fact, that we can be real with God. We don't have to worry about criticism or fear rejection when we come to him.

Psalm 51, David's confession to God after being confronted about his sin with Bathsheba, is beautiful in its truth:

> Generous in love—God, give grace! Huge in mercy—
> wipe out my bad record.
> Scrub away my guilt,
> soak out my sins in your laundry.
> I know how bad I've been;
> my sins are staring me down. . . .
> What you're after is truth from the inside out.
> (vv. 1–3, 6 MSG)

Truth from the inside out. Just as I am. Once and for real. That's what I wanted for myself. But how would I do it?

The Real You

Think about this: the God of the universe, the Creator of all that is, seen and unseen, has already seen the absolute

worst you've got to offer. He knows every lie you've ever told, every lie you've ever believed about yourself. He knows the deepest, most hidden secret of your heart. He knows it all, and he loves you just as you are. If you could really believe that what he says about you is true, how would it change the way you live? Imagine yourself being totally loved and totally accepted despite all your mistakes and flaws. How would your life be different?

A Prayer for Posers

Thomas Merton, a monk who earnestly sought to be real with God, once said, "The reason we never enter into the deepest reality of our relationship with God is that we so seldom acknowledge our utter nothingness before him."

Make that your confession today as you pray this prayer:

"Father God, I confess that without you, I'm nothing but a poser. A picture-perfect fake. A fraud. Apart from you, I can do nothing, and I can be nothing that is real and true. Thank you for inviting me to come to you so long ago. Thank you for letting me come back to you again and again. Thank you for rescuing me from myself. Amen."

Just Like You: Young Women Who Touched the World
Rahab and the Woman at the Well: Bad Girls Make Good

Through the ages, God has delighted in making helpers out of the unlikeliest candidates—people who seem to be the least qualified for the job.

The book of Joshua describes how God used Rahab, a prostitute in Jericho, to help the Israelites during the time of Moses. Rahab had heard the stories of how God had delivered the Israelites out of Pharaoh's hands in Egypt and how God had brought low all those who opposed them. When Israelite spies appeared at her door, Rahab knew Jericho's walls would eventually fall to their God. She hid the spies from her king and helped them secretly escape in order to ensure the survival of her family.

Her obedience to the mighty God of Israel saved Rahab. And this same God took care of her family for generations to come. In the New Testament, she is listed in the lineage of Jesus himself (see Matthew 1). The book of Hebrews also mentions her and her act of faith: "By faith the harlot Rahab perished not with them that believed not, when she had received the spies with peace" (11:31 KJV).

God did not look at Rahab as a prostitute or even as a sinner. He simply saw her as someone who recognized who he was and who his people were. She was justified in his sight by her willingness to take care of the Israelites.

Then the New Testament tells the story of the woman at the well. She was a Samaritan woman who had had several husbands and lovers and was currently living with a man who was not her husband. She came to the well one day and found Jesus waiting for her. They talked, and he told her, "Go and sin no more."

The story, told in John 4, describes how this woman, after her encounter with Jesus, ran and proclaimed to her people the good news of the One who had offered her "living water."

These are just two of the "least likely" that God drafted into his service. The Bible teems with stories of others. Do you think you're not qualified to be used by God to fulfill his purposes? Think again!

chapter three

Glass House,
Airbrushed Soul

Painted on,
Life is behind a mask.
Self-inflicted circus clown,
I'm tired of the song and dance.

I have freckles. I mean, I'm not totally freckled, but I have them. They have taken up permanent residence on the bridge of my nose, and unfortunately, due to my desire as a teenager to be the "blonde, tanned bombshell," they decided to move on down to my chest and shoulders as well.

As a little girl, I remember thinking freckles were my kisses from the sun. They made me cute, fresh-faced—the girl next door, right? Wrong.

Sometimes I wondered how I could ever have considered

those freckles as beauty marks! Then, a few years later, came my first professional photo shoot, and the true extent of my freckles impairment was glaringly revealed.

It was a big day for me. I was finally living my dream, I had a record deal, I was making music, and now I was going to have the pictures to prove it all. We were at a beautiful house in Topanga Canyon, near Los Angeles, and it was like a scene out of movie—the photographer, the stylist, the manager, the director. There was a lot of commotion. Wow! I never knew a girl needed so many people to have her picture taken.

Once again I was the center of attention, and this time I really felt like a star—right up until everyone started talking about me as if I weren't there. But I *was* there, and I heard everything.

"We can use these pants to make her look taller and this light to make her look thinner and this angle to diminish her round face," they were saying. And of course those awful freckles had to be hidden.

The voice in my head screamed, *I can hear you! I'm right here. Can't you see me?*

But then my inner monologue quieted and began to reason. *Well, I'd better just keep quiet. I'm so blessed to be here. I mean, thousands of girls would give anything to trade places with me, right? Maybe I shouldn't have had that bagel for breakfast; bread makes you bloated, or so I've heard. I need to throw up. Just a little, just once. I need a release, just a quick one.*

My head was spinning. I felt out of control and closed in. I excused myself, made my way to the bathroom, expelled the food from my stomach . . . and felt as though I'd gained back a bit of control.

I know I shouldn't have done that, but . . .

The old excuses, the old low-self-esteem head talk, started up again. Then I vowed, *I'll do better tomorrow.*

I headed back to my dressing room, and the makeup artist began her work on my face. As she painted away, she said matter-of-factly, "Wow. You have large pores."

I guess I do. I mean, I knew that, but I never gave it much thought. Until now.

"I have a great concealer for your freckles. But hey, that's what Photoshop is for. Whatever I don't clear up they can airbrush out on the computer," she said flippantly.

After twelve grueling hours of being poked, prodded, and painted, the charade parade finally ended, and what few morsels of positive self-image I might have started out with that morning were long gone.

REAL GIRL, REAL LIFE

Dreaming in Color

When asked what might make her happy, Dadra points to a television show that illustrates the kind of life she some-day hopes to lead.

"I like *Lizzie McGuire*," she says admiringly. "Hilary Duff has a whole lot of friends; she has a good life."

But when challenged with the notion that Duff's television adventures are not real, Dadra is quick to set the record straight. "Yes, they *are* real," she insists. "Her school is across from that radio station right here in town."

Regardless of where Hilary Duff actually lives, for now this reflective sixth grader must settle for a life that is a world away from that of *Lizzie McGuire*. One of seven children, Dadra lives in a housing project with her parents, her siblings, her aunt and uncle and their twin two-year-olds, and two dogs. She shares a small bedroom with four other girls, a situation that doesn't seem to bother her. The hardest part about being eleven, she says, is stepping up to the increased responsibility that comes with her age.

"Sometimes I don't watch the kids like I'm told to, and I get yelled at," she confesses. "On Fridays, my mom, my auntie, and my uncle all leave. Then my three older sisters go to the dance. I have to stay home and watch five kids: one is nine, one is seven, one is five, and then the two-year-old twins. It makes me feel sad when they yell at me because I'm the only one there, and I have so much to do. I have to clean up the house and change the diapers, and I can't get it all done."

Though she feels the weight of her family obligations, Dadra still finds time to do homework, watch TV, play outside, and dream of what her life would be like if she were given the same opportunities as Lizzie McGuire. "My life would be just like a movie," she asserts. "I would be able to get out of the house and actually do something with my life. The number one thing I want to do with my life is sing and dance and be in videos and stuff. It would give me the money to get a house and some food. I really want to be famous. I want people to come up to me and say, 'Give me your autograph!' That would make me feel like a new woman. I could say, 'The old girl is gone. Here comes the new one.'"

Just like Dadra, sometimes our dreams are the only things that get us through the reality of today—the hard stuff of life. Our dreams grow up as we grow up, as God opens our eyes to what matters in this life.

SMOKE AND MIRRORS

How well I remember seeing the first "finished" picture after that photo shoot. I walked into my record company's office, and there it was, printed out as a large, glossy eight by ten.

The girl in the photo was beautiful. I mean, her face was flawless. With every freckle magically missing, every pore resized, that girl's complexion was porcelain perfect. I couldn't take my eyes off her.

But who was she? I could only see glimpses of what was

left of Natalie. The photo experts had not only airbrushed my face; they had airbrushed away a little piece of my soul. As I looked into the girl's eyes for signs of life, I felt so hollow.

Don't let it show, Natalie, the voice inside whispered. *Keep it together.*

I pasted on my plastic smile and told everyone I loved it. "Wow," I said. "I look beautiful."

But I left there feeling emptier than ever.

> *People are like stained glass windows—the true beauty can be seen only when there is light from within. The darker the night, the brighter the windows.*
>
> —Elisabeth Kübler-Ross[2]

A BLESSING AND A CURSE

It was the coolest thing ever to hear my song on the radio for the first time. I felt like a rock star. And standing on stage, doing what I love and hearing the audience sing along to songs I have written, is one of life's greatest gifts.

But success comes with a price. Truth is, being a professional singer is not all it's cracked up to be.

There are tremendous pressures on young women in the music industry, especially young women focused on straight-ahead, positive, pop music. Maybe it's all in my mind, but it seems the pressure on girls who have "big" voices is that they must have a "big" image. I've never been into that whole diva thing. In fact, I've always wished I could be a bit more of the earthy, folksy, sling-a-guitar-over-my-shoulder, only-shave-my-legs-every-couple-of-weeks, dirty-hair kind of singer/songwriter, content to share my music with the attitude, Who cares about my image? But I'm not quite that artsy.

Then there is the added pressure of being a *Christian* recording artist, a blessing that can also be a curse. It's a blessing for me because I sing about what truly matters to me. And it is such a privilege when I'm given the opportunity to speak encouragement into another person's life. But it's a curse too, because if you wear the label, people expect you to have your life together and to be able to provide spiritually correct answers for all life's problems. You need an ever-ready supply of memorized Scripture passages that offer encouragement for those who are dealing with a marriage on the rocks, a child who's into drugs, a financial setback that has wrecked the family, an illness that has weakened their faith, or a host of other crises. You also need the perfect theological explanation for the cynic and a smiley-face, you-can-do-it attitude to encourage the aspiring young Christian singer. I consistently feel the pressure to always be *on*. I can't be tired, I can't be sad, I can't just be *not* in the mood.

So here's what it comes down to: I have to be beautiful and pimple-free yet humble and Christ-centered. I have to point others to the cross while making sure I never, ever mess up enough to need the grace that cross represents. I have to be fashion-forward and hip, always wearing the latest trends, but I absolutely must fit everyone's idea of modesty. Finally, I must be able to recite the recipe for this perfect life by quoting all the right Scripture verses.

You're thinking, *Natalie, no one would ever expect all that of you!*

I would argue that yes, indeed, there *was* someone who expected all that and more. It's what *I* expected of myself.

Why had I created this ideal person in my mind, and why did I think I had to live up to such impossible perfection? Because I believed that anything less from me would be a tremendous disappointment to my family, my friends, my fans. As a dyed-in-the-wool people pleaser, I would do everything in my power to keep that from happening.

The most difficult part of attaining perfection is finding something to do for an encore.

—Author Unknown

And that, of course, was the real problem. I was plugged in to the wrong power source.

A Symptom of Struggle

I confess: I am a perfectionist. Research suggests that girls who are most vulnerable to eating disorders are perfectionists, anxious to please, and compulsive.

Hel-loooo! That would be me. If my life were a survey and these characteristics were listed, I would have to mark "(d) all of the above"!

As obvious as it may seem to "outsiders," it's not always easy for the person trapped in some kind of destructive behavior, like forced vomiting, to figure out that the behavior is driven by a faulty self-image. That's one reason that it's so hard to break the habitual behavior. Until the underlying issues are exposed and addressed, it's almost impossible to stop the overwhelming urges.

My struggle with bulimia was only a symptom of a deeper emotional and spiritual struggle gripping the core of my heart and mind, but the problem continued until I understood that link. To conquer the disorder, I would have to unleash those turbulent issues of the heart. It wouldn't be pretty, and the journey would take me down a winding, unfamiliar, and sometimes frightening path. But along the way I found the honesty, vulnerability, and self-examination that would ultimately lead to my healing.

Realizing What Really Matters

Sometimes I feel like the world is made up of two kinds of people: people pleasers (those who so need to be loved and accepted that they go to great lengths to be loved and yet never feel they deserve it), and people who are never pleased with anything (those from whom the pleasers try so desperately to get love and attention but who can't seem to see beyond their own wants and needs).

Know what I mean?

Whether it's true or whether it's just the voice of cynicism babbling in my head, it's fair to say that those two categories of people don't just pop into being when they enter adolescence. The pleasers learn from a very early age—in part through parenting or lack thereof—to bury their own feelings, to accept responsibility for anything that goes wrong, or to think they should be able to fix any troublesome situation that arises for their loved ones. On the other hand, people who are never pleased with anything tend to be just the opposite: their feelings are the most important in any situation, they are never to blame for anything that goes wrong, and they would never bother trying to fix what is not their fault.

My friend Agnes would be the first to admit she's been a people pleaser all her life. She said, "When I was a child, I remember thinking, *If I could just be a better girl, maybe my mom wouldn't be so worried all the time. Or maybe Daddy wouldn't work so much.*

"That thinking translated over into my teenage years when I worked hard to be one of the cool girls that the boys would pay attention to. In college, I became an overachiever, killing myself for an A+ because an A simply wouldn't do. But the older I get, and the more I begin to understand the kind of life God created me for and how little that has to do with what other people think of me, the more I understand how futile being a people pleaser is."

In Ephesians 4:17, the apostle Paul talks about those who live "in the futility of their mind" (NKJV); they spend more time trying to know what others want from them than they do in pursuing knowledge of God. When we spend all our energy trying to earn another person's affections, trying to do all we can do and being all we can be for another human, our lives are sucked up in an endless vacuum.

We were created for more than a desperate search for approval and acceptance, for more than a life of fear. God told his children in Isaiah 43:1, "Now this is what the LORD says. He created you, people of Jacob; he formed you, people of Israel. He says, 'Don't be afraid, because I have saved you. I have called you by name, and you are mine.'"

That message is for his children—for us!

We've not been placed on this planet to be people pleasers. We are accepted and loved by the One who created and rescued us. Nothing else matters except returning that love back to him in the way we love others and in the way we love and care for ourselves. In that, he is well pleased (see 1 Thessalonians 2:4).

The Real You

Think about it. Are you a classic people pleaser, as described earlier? Or are you a person who is rarely pleased with anything? In the space below, write about your "people-pleasing" experiences and how they have impacted you, either as the pleaser or the impossible-to-please person.

Now take a moment to pray one of these prayers:

If you're a pleaser, pray, "God, being a people pleaser is sucking the life out of me. Help me to believe your Word, to accept that you've called me by name and that I am yours. With all my heart, mind, and soul, I want to please you and only you. Amen."

If you lean more toward being the rarely-pleased-with-anything type, be brave and pray this prayer: "Lord, it's no surprise to you how picky I am. As much as I'd like to be different, I'm a perfectionist. I want things the way I want them, and I can be pretty critical and judgmental of people who aren't like me. But I'd like to be different. I really want to be happy and thankful. I believe you can help me. Amen."

Just Like You: Young Women Who Touched the World

India.Arie: Believe in Love

When India.Arie learned how to play the guitar in seventh grade, she had no idea what kind of impact she was going to have on the music scene or popular culture. She was simply a girl who loved music.

Growing up as the child of celebrities (her mother was a Motown singer and her father a professional basketball player), India.Arie was always surrounded by her family's encouragement. "Both my mom and dad encouraged me, but once I started singing, my mom was my mentor," she says. "She grew up in Detroit when Motown was new, and she taught me everything about singing and songwriting."

When she was twenty-one, India.Arie decided to take her amazing musical talent public, and she moved to Atlanta to pursue a music career. Her work was immediately and enthusiastically received. Her 2001 release, Acoustic Soul, sold more than a million copies, and the projects that followed have been successful as well.

Despite her success, she still gets nervous every time she goes onstage. "The only reason I started performing is that I believed in my songs. My songs are very introspective, and I sing from my heart. It's very real," she says.

The songs that India.Arie believes in so much are ones she writes herself. She stands out in a crowd because her music is so powerful. The essence of everything she writes is this: Love yourself! She believes that love and faith can move mountains—that we can become our best selves when we learn to see ourselves as the beloved daughters and sons of a creative, loving God. The power of that message is what has made a shy girl brave enough to perform before millions of listeners.

chapter four

The Myth of Me

Living a charade,
I'm always on parade.
What a mess I've made of my existence,
But you love me even now.

Although I never felt it until recently, I was always told that I am unique. My parents, teacher after teacher, spiritual mentors, and others have all confirmed that I am the only me. These respected adults would speak of my unmatched potential and the fact that my Creator knows the number of hairs on my head. They told me God knew me before the world was made. They reminded me that no one else has my DNA and that my fingerprints are one of a kind.

It's not as though I thought these people were lying to

me. I knew they believed what they were telling me, and deep down I knew there must be some truth to it all. But I just couldn't accept what they were saying.

Well, it's not really that I wasn't able to accept it. I just wasn't ready. Everything they said, though birthed from beautiful and pure motives, fell on deaf ears. I was either distracted by the ugly voice in my head, the voice that sounded just like my own and whispered lies filled with doubt and self-hatred, or I was simply too busy—too busy trying to be someone else instead of listening to anyone urging me to be my unique self.

The Real You

Quick! List two things you do almost every day to hide the real you—things you do to ensure that others don't figure out what you don't want them to know. What does that mask look like when you're at school, at work, or at the mall? Do you dare to think about what might happen if you decide to take it off? If you're brave enough, write about it here:

1.

2.

All the comparing, all the pretending, all the people pleasing—it was an exhausting charade that took every ounce of energy I had. But there was no quitting the game because *I* was the game. Without the facade, I would be nothing; I would cease to exist—or so I thought. I was fed up with being a fake, with functioning as someone I wasn't. But I didn't know how to stop trying so hard and simply become real. I didn't know what I would become if I stopped living the lie.

The guilt was unbearable at times. As I stood on church platforms—leading others, quoting Scripture, repeating the same truths my parents and others had told me about how God made us all unique and special, reminding audience members that they too had a divine destiny—feelings of guilt swept over me as the promises of God came out of my mouth. Incredibly, I was urging others to believe the very truths I myself did not accept.

Sometimes I wondered, *How can I possibly be a Christian yet be so uncomfortable in my own skin?*

Your beauty and love chase after me every day of my life. (Psalm 23:6 MSG)

What Matters Most

On paper, Stephanie looks like your classic high achiever. She's the historian of the student council and cohistorian for the National Honor Society. She's a member of the Spanish Club; the Spanish Honor Society; the orchestra; the mathematics honor society, Mu Alpha Theta; and Impact, the school club dedicated to community service. And as though all that wasn't enough, she signed up for all the Advanced Placement classes her school offers and became a social officer on her dance team.

The truth is, Stephanie, the daughter of Korean immigrants, has more than one reason for staying so busy.

"From about seventh grade until about the end of my sophomore year in high school I was really driven to achieve," she confesses. "If I didn't meet the standard I set for myself—which was often perfection—it caused my self-esteem to plummet. Sometimes even making 100 on a test wasn't enough. I thought I should've gotten the bonus points."

At the end of her sophomore year, Stephanie had a major shift in perspective, due largely to some personal Bible study and godly soul searching. "I realized that getting good grades and winning awards were not nearly as important as the things that were going on in the lives of those around me," she says. "I had been spending so much time studying or practicing the things I wanted to excel in that I wasn't spending very much time with God or with the people I care about. Every night when I'd look back on my day, I realized that 90 percent was school—you know, studying that extra hour so I could do well on a test and such. And I think that has really hurt me, in a way, because in the long run it's not about my grades.

"I have friends whose parents put a lot of pressure on them to succeed academically," she continues, "and it's really hard on them. That's really sad to me because what are they going to say when God wants to know what they did with their life? That they made As in all their classes? That's not the legacy I want to leave. Sure, I love to learn, and I want to do all things excellently, but I hope that what motivates me the most to be involved in so many things is the desire to love and impact people. That's where my focus is now."

BEYOND BELIEF

Certainly I *was* a Christian—and had been for a long time. I first met Jesus when I was six years old. It happened in my basement on a soggy, Seattle night. There was no hum of the organ while a teary-eyed preacher begged for one last soul. Just my mom folding laundry while the fresh scent of Downy floated through the air. Right there, next to the blue, plastic clothesbasket filled with fresh towels and a few socks, my mother took my small hand and led me in the sinner's prayer. I was quite young, but I had sat through "big" church enough to hear it all. And although on that night there was no fiery message of fear promising hell and damnation to all who did not believe, I must admit it was probably my worries of being eternally separated from my family and my aversion to burning forever in a lake of fire that led me to ask, "Mommy, when I die, will I go to heaven?"

Afterward, with the assurance that "when the roll is called up yonder," my name will be on it, I went about life as usual, doing what all good Christians do—learning Scripture, serving in the church, and getting a lot of pats on the back along the way.

By the time I reached my college years, I had a whole lot of head knowledge but very little heart knowledge. I often wondered, *Is this all there is to the Christian life?* Maybe that tiny thought was the root of my identity crisis. I was asking the questions but not arriving at any answers. Although I was full of religion and piety, I felt empty.

God cannot give us happiness and peace apart from himself, because it is not there. There is no such thing.

—C. S. Lewis

Packing It On

My freshman year in college turned out to be a pivotal one. By now the mask of perfection was firmly in place, and the fraud I was living earned me much attention and won me many friends. I enjoyed, even indulged, in a certain amount of popularity. And as many college freshmen do, I also indulged in horrible eating habits. Thanks to a daily Froot Loop ritual in the dining hall (college cafeterias are truly gross, aren't they?) and my affection for late-night pizzas and greasy fast food, I packed on the dreaded "freshman fifteen" in a hurry.

Oddly enough, I believed at the time that I had even that situation under control. In spite of the fact that I was becoming a little, uh, *fluffy*, I had never willingly purged. I was hanging on by a thread but still felt I was successfully manipulating the circumstances and relationships in my life so as to keep everything under control. It required a serious balancing act to manage classes and studying, cheerleading, and traveling with the college music ministry team. And of course, I had to be the best at all of it to keep my sense of identity.

The only thing missing from my perfect life was the perfect boy. I was, after all, attending Bible college, otherwise known as bridal college. Rarely did a girl escape without her Mrs. degree.

I had been a serial dater from the time I was legal, which in my parents' home was age sixteen. Confidence is attractive, no matter how artificial it is, so I never had a hard time getting a date. I had experienced a lot of puppy love in high school, but now I was ready for the real deal. I had lots of friends but still felt lonely. Turns out most of those friends were really just acquaintances, people who thought they knew me well but didn't. After all, I was the master controller, and I only let each person in so far.

Certain that true love would be different, I told myself I would be fearless, I would love freely, and in that relationship I would feel safe to discover who I really am, without pretense or expectation. Desperate to be understood, I was convinced that true love would fill the void I had felt for so long. And I was right. Well, right and wrong too. True love could do that, but it wouldn't come in the form I expected. I thought it would feel familiar, like something I thought I already knew well. But in reality, I knew very little about love. Meanwhile, it stood waiting to take me by surprise, an emotion more passionate than I'd ever imagined, more real and precious than any I'd ever known.

GETTING REAL WITH GOD:
THE ORIGINAL, WONDERFUL YOU

Why Settle for Less Than the You God Created You to Be?

Ashamedly, I must admit, while flipping through the TV channels one night, I allowed myself to become engrossed in an MTV reality show called *I Want a Famous Face*. Horrified,

I watched as twin teenage brothers endured unimaginable pain through several surgeries while doctors attempted to fulfill their impossible dream of having their faces reformed to resemble Brad Pitt's.

While I respect their taste in faces (Brad is easy to look at), most disturbing to me was their deep desire to give up their own identity and become someone else. They were in the driver's seat of their lives and believed they would get everything they ever wanted if they could just remake their physical appearance.

Of course, the end result did not give the world two more Brad Pitts, and the Band-Aid the boys put on their insecurities will only cause their wounds to fester and grow. While I pray none of you will go to such great lengths to find approval and acceptance, many of us attempt to recreate ourselves daily by focusing on outward appearance or by pursuing personal achievements that bring awards, relationships, and so on. Our identity becomes wrapped up in trying to be what society defines as success instead of what God deems as successful.

The world says, Look out for yourself. God says, Serve others.

The world says, Beauty is important. God says, I look at your heart.

The world says, Be first in line. God says, The last shall be first.

As life rolls along, it's hard for us to stay in the passenger seat; we want to control our destiny. And I guess to some extent we do, because we must choose to follow Christ. Once we do that, letting him lead isn't easy, but it's essential to finding ourselves and fulfilling our destiny.

As your insecurities and hidden fears come bubbling to the surface, don't shove them back down and cover them up with the world's temporary fixes. Embrace them, knowing that as you do, healing will come as you find yourself in Christ. Don't try to be anyone but you. There's only one Brad Pitt, and there's only one you. You're an original with a God-sized destiny. So move over, because he's the only one with a license to drive your life.

Here's one for the road, a truth for the journey ahead: "You made my whole being; you formed me in my mother's body. I praise you because you made me in an amazing and wonderful way. What you have done is wonderful. I know this very well" (Psalm 139:13–14).

Maybe you're not convinced yet, but hang in there; with God's help, you can be.

The Real You

So what about you? What part of yourself have you lost while pursuing society's definition of beauty and success?

What have you given up? What lengths have you gone to in pursuit of beauty and acceptance? Quick! Don't think too much about the answers; just write down your off-the-cuff thoughts to answer those questions. Then, when you're done, ask yourself honestly, *What has my time on this runway cost me?*

Think about it.

God is our Creator. God made us in his image and likeness. Therefore we are creators . . . the joy of creativeness should be ours.

—Dorothy Day

Mary: Let It Be to Me As You Have Said

Did you know that Mary, the mother of Jesus, was only *thirteen* years old when the angel of the Lord came to visit her and told her she would give birth to the Son of God?

"How can this be?" Mary asked, confused because she was a virgin.

The angel replied, "The Holy Spirit will come upon you, and the power of the Most High will overshadow you. So the Holy One to be born will be called the Son of God."

Mary swallowed her fear and then answered the angel with all the faith she had within her: "I am the Lord's servant. Let it be to me as you have said."

She knew this strange and wonderful announcement from God could mean trouble for her. After all, Mary was engaged. What would her fiancé, Joseph, say? Would he believe her? If he didn't, he could have her stoned to death! Her whole life could be ruined by this visitation from God.

Young Mary must have been afraid, but instead of rejecting the marvelous promise of God that she would bear his Son, she praised God for all she didn't understand. Her words, recorded in the first chapter of the Gospel of Luke and quoted here from the New International Version, are read by millions now. She said, "My soul glorifies the Lord and my spirit rejoices in God my

Savior, for he has been mindful of the humble state of his servant. From now on all generations will call me blessed."

Mary's faith sustained her despite all the risks. God went before her and revealed his plan to Joseph. Her life was saved, and she gave birth to Jesus. All around the world, we know her as the one who said yes to God, and her example gives us hope that we can do the same.

chapter five

From Prince Charming to Pandora's Box

But you see the real me,
Hiding in my skin,
Broken from within.
Unveil me completely;
I'm loosening my grasp.
There's no need to mask my frailty
'Cause you see the real me.

*M*y college experience took a fantastic turn when I met Prince Charming.

Mr. Tall-Dark-and-Handsome drove a red sports car and was the epitome of cool. When he smiled, I swear I could see the twinkle and hear that *ding!* sound effect that I thought was only possible in toothpaste commercials or Disney movies. He was the man of every girl's dream, the big man on campus admired by all the girls. I giggled at the very sight of him. He was so beautiful.

At first I didn't recognize the warm yet nervous feelings

I had when I looked at him, maybe because I had never felt anything quite like them before. I wondered if he would even notice me, the young little freshman. Still, I was hopeful. Word had been getting around about my vocal talent, so I held out hope that maybe, just maybe, he knew about me.

Then one day, out of nowhere, he sought me out.

The Real You

Let's talk about boys. Guys. The male species. Face it, we love guys. And that's quite OK. God made us for love. To love and worship him and to love and be loved by the right guy.

But along the way to finding the right guy, the prince of our dreams, some of us wind up kissing a lot of toads. We do a lot of stupid things, hoping upon hope just to be noticed. In the space below—c'mon, now, be brave!—write down the lengths you've gone to, to win a guy's attention. Then ask yourself why.

There I sat, in the cafeteria with my friends, eating my usual bowl of Froot Loops (much more appetizing than the mystery meat they called chicken), when I saw him across the crowded room. (I always saw him because I was always on the lookout for him.)

Then it hit me. He wasn't just walking through the cafeteria. He was headed straight for *me*.

Why do I have on my oversized sweatshirt today? I look so frumpy, I fumed to myself. Of course this would also be the day I had decided to go "natural" and not wear a stitch of makeup. My palms began to sweat, a family of butterflies started fluttering in my stomach, and nature's blush found its way to my cheeks.

Turns out he knew a couple of the girls sitting with me, so he sat down. I'm unsure whether he just came over to say hello to my friends or if he was interested in meeting me, but in that moment I didn't care. He looked into my eyes and introduced himself. From the moment I heard him utter one word, I could tell he was a confident man of strength, one who knew how to take control and lead.

All that from a quick hello, you ask?

Yes, all that and so much more. I had *never* felt like that before.

The Ultimate in Perfection

And so it began. That passing introduction soon led to many beautiful moments of discovery as we shared our dreams for the future and discussed life's deepest questions.

So this is what it's like to be in love, I marveled. I liked it; I *loved* it. Hours of phone calls and our daily cafeteria rendezvous—just me, my newfound soul mate, and my Froot Loops.

He knew so much Scripture, he was so well read, and he always knew just the right thing to say and when to say it. He was intimidating, but in an intoxicating way that challenged me and made me want to be better.

I was in love, but my prince's high expectations presented a whole new problem to my already fragile psyche. The pressure for perfection I had struggled with my whole life intensified in my relationship.

I must hold on to this at any price, my mind repeated in an endless chorus. *I can't mess this up. I have to be everything he needs, and if I am not, I'll find out what he needs and become that.*

Truth was, I wasn't the only one who found him to be the ultimate in male perfection. Turns out he believed it as well.

He was used to being a champion, but I guess he felt

he didn't have enough trophies. *I would be his crowning achievement.* When he asked me to marry him, I should have listened to that still, small voice inside me that asked, *Are you sure this is your forever?*

REAL GIRL, REAL LIFE

Before the Boys . . .

Stevie says she's never been the boy-crazy type, but if you push her ever so slightly on the subject she will admit to having been a little too crazy about one boy in particular.

"There's a guy I was really into, and we were on again, off again throughout middle school," remembers Stevie, now sixteen. "If I look back and honestly evaluate our relationship, I'd have to say that most of the time I was just trying to impress him and get his attention. After we broke up for the last time, he started dating some of my friends, and I was so jealous it made me miserable at times. It took awhile, but I had to grow out of that."

Not that this lively, vivacious identical twin has lost all desire to be noticed by the opposite sex. It's just that she's realized there's more to romantic relationships than pounding hearts and starry eyes. "My friends and I are always saying, 'I want a boyfriend! I want a boyfriend!'" she admits. "Of course I want a boyfriend; all girls want a boyfriend! We want that companionship. But I don't need a boyfriend. All the guys I know—sure, they're cute, they're nice, but they're not what I'm looking for. The guy I'm looking for will like me for who I am, not for the kind of clothes or makeup I wear. He'll also understand my priorities in life."

Stevie's priorities are her family and getting settled into college so she can one day fulfill her dream of being a teacher. "Realistically, I may not have a whole lot of time to spend with a boyfriend," she continues, "because I need to work on my own goals. That's the point of these years—to get to know myself—and then I can add a boyfriend into the mix. You have to find yourself before you can truly be with somebody else."

Opening Pandora's Box

I had strong feelings for my fiancé, but I worried that forever love was supposed to be *more* than what I was feeling—more intense, more reassuring. But if I broke off our relationship, it would mean I had failed. And I couldn't bear the thought of failure.

Yet I knew something was wrong. There were oh-so-subtle hints that showed how little he valued me. For instance, I'd see him slip out of church while I was up front singing a solo. It was obvious that he believed God's plan was that a wife was to support her husband in all *his* endeavors and dreams, not the other way around.

He was always quick to point out my inadequacies, spiritual and otherwise. Being under his spiritual microscope made me feel as though whatever Scripture I did know hadn't been interpreted correctly. And he hinted that my spiritual experience wasn't real.

Then it happened. I don't know who she was, but the only thing more beautiful than her long, shiny, toned and tanned legs was her flawless face. There she was on the cover of a magazine in the grocery-store checkout lane, the essence of pure perfection.

"Now *that's* what I call beautiful," he said, staring at the wonder girl. I hated her, and I didn't even know her name. She represented everything I wasn't, and she had the very thing I wanted: his approval. Later, as he asked me (and not for the first time) if I was keeping up my workouts, something cracked in me. We made our way to our favorite Mexican restaurant, and with the image of "Brazilian-babe" still fresh in my mind, I decided to have a light lunch—a small salad. I really wasn't that hungry, so maybe I shouldn't have eaten at all, but I did.

Then I excused myself to go to the restroom, and there, in a tiny stall, I opened Pandora's Box.

It was quite easy, really. Much easier than I thought it would be, and I liked it because, in a strange way, it made me feel in control. Best of all, he didn't know about it. No one had to know. It was my very own thing.

After that, one day turned into the next and then the next, and every day I was purging. Eventually, throwing up became a way of life. I had become a bulimic, borderline anorexic. I wasn't a classic bulimic who binged on large amounts of food and then purged. Instead, I threw up what little bit of nourishment I was putting into my body. I believed not a single ounce of food, not one calorie, healthy or not, could stay. I had to get rid of it.

Within a year, my weight dropped below one hundred pounds.

In the perverse way anorexics see themselves, my body, though gaunt and very thin, began to resemble those I saw in magazines, movies, and on television. I actually thought I looked good. And apparently others thought so too. In fact, as a result of the weight loss, I got so much positive feedback and affirmation, I felt assured that I had gained some control back. The compliments empowered me. The relationship with Mr. Everything was zapping away what little sense of self I had, but he couldn't take *this* away.

This secret was mine. I owned it, and I was holding on to it for dear life.

Every happening, great and small, is a parable whereby God speaks to us, and the art of life is to get the message.
—Malcolm Muggeridge

Kneeling to the Wrong God

All the weakness and insecurity I had struggled with for most of my years had come to a crashing crescendo. I had been searching for the answer to "Who am I?" my whole life, and now I had given my heart so easily to one who handled it so carelessly. I'd given up the search for myself in order to seek the answer to "Who does he want me to be?"

And then something changed. All the positive attention I was receiving as a result of my newly svelte figure gave me the courage to dump Prince Charming.

That was a positive thing, a change for the better. But there was a negative side too. The spotlight on my appearance sent me sliding down a treacherous slope, and I couldn't find the brakes. I thought my secret purging was giving me control, but in fact, I was in bondage. For eighteen long months, I didn't even know I was sick. My hair was falling out, my teeth were horribly discolored, and I was getting so thin my face looked sunken. Still, bulimia held a blinding power over me. The positive attention about my weight loss that I'd initially received from my family and friends soon turned to concern; yet somehow this, too, was strangely exhilarating.

Then the acid from my constant purging began to affect the quality of my voice. So much of my identity was wrapped up in my talent as a singer that I couldn't bear the thought of my voice being damaged. I guess God knew that was the one thing that would get my attention. It was enough, anyway, to get me to give my destructive diet plan a rest. So for six months, I managed not to purge.

But the purging wasn't the real problem. In reality, the physical act of vomiting was just a destructive symptom of a much greater issue I had not truly come to terms with. It was still hidden away like a ghost under my bed, just waiting for the right moment to devour me.

I know what I'm doing. I have it all planned out—plans to take care of you, not abandon you, plans to give you the future you hope for. (Jeremiah 29:11 MSG)

The confrontation came on a Thursday night. I had moved back into my parents' house for a semester, and we had just finished dinner when I heard a knock on the door. There stood my brother and three sisters with love in their hearts and concern in their eyes.

They hadn't let me know they were coming. I guess they thought if they took me by surprise, I wouldn't have time to make up any lies to answer their questions. They were worried about me. My sister Jennifer was carrying a book with information on bulimia. She and the rest of my family lovingly yet directly asked me if I was a bulimic. My secret was out.

Or was it?

Responding to my family's gentle confrontation, a *part* of my problem came out as I poured out the lurid details of my damaging romance, explaining how it had knocked me down to nothing. But even then, I was still the master of ceremonies, determined to stay in control and only divulging what I wanted them to know. I assured them I had successfully conquered my eating disorder and was on my way to health and restoration.

Seeing the delight and relief in their eyes, I wanted to say more, keep the feeling going. *Tell them everything!* the voice in my head screamed.

I can't, came the reply.

Tell them you're NOT a tough girl and that this whole I've-got-it-all-together routine is just an act.

And He said to me, "My grace is sufficient for you, for My strength is made perfect in weakness." Therefore most gladly I will rather boast in my infirmities, that the power of Christ may rest upon me. (2 Corinthians 12:9–10 NKJV)

Again the other part of me argued, *I can't.*

Tell them you're deathly afraid of failure and how desperately you want to please them.

I can't, I can't, I can't!

The evening ended, and we parted with lots of hugs, love, and encouragement. But over the next few weeks, slowly but surely, the image I obsessed over in the mirror led me back down that familiar path, and soon I was purging again. This on again, off again behavior would continue to control me through the next five years of my life.

Spending so much time on my knees in front of the porcelain throne, would I ever realize I was kneeling to the wrong god?

Yet still the true God knocked on the door of my heart.

He never gave up.

He never walked away in disgust.

Jesus was still pursuing me.

Our patient Savior gently but continuously knocked. The deadbolt was unlocked, and I had cracked open the door a bit, but I could not release the safety chain and swing it open wide. Although I could see his light shining through the keyhole, I still chose to hide in the dark corner of my insecurity and unbelief. He knew this, and he patiently waited.

A Fine, Porcelain Place to Begin

On the day of my initial breakthrough, as I lay in a crumpled heap around the base of that toilet, I finally realized I had come to the end of myself. In that cold, lonely moment, the Spirit of God fell upon me like a warm, comforting blanket.

I recognized his voice. It came into my head like an old, familiar Friend, and I could sense him whisper to me these words of life: *My grace is sufficient for you, for my strength is made perfect in weakness.*

In that moment I began to understand how truly weak I was. My secret failures had finally caught up with me, but I didn't have to hide my frailties any longer. In fact, I could celebrate them, because in doing so I would allow Christ's strength to come into its own and accomplish a work that only he could do. It was a concept I would never have accepted before but now, for the first time, was able to consider.

With tear-soaked eyes and the smell of vomit on my breath, I was held in the arms of my Savior. I knew wholeness wouldn't come overnight, but I was blessed that day to take the first step. God opened my eyes just enough for me to see that I was worth more than what was visible on the outside. He was showing me that underneath the crude, harsh portrait I'd scribbled of myself there was another, truer portrait. For the first time, I was able to see that he was creating a masterpiece, and that masterpiece was *me*. From the tattered fibers of my life he was weaving what would one day become a perfect tapestry.

GETTING REAL WITH GOD: MORE THAN ENOUGH

No Matter How Crazy Life Gets, God Is in Control

Music is so powerful it can sometimes speak the truth like nothing else. In the early days of my music career, I joined a traveling musical group called Truth. It sometimes felt like music boot camp as we performed around three hundred concerts a year.

One of those concerts found me back in Seattle, onstage at my home church. I remember how great it was to look out and see the faces of my family as I performed with Truth. However, there was one particular face that night that grabbed my attention like no other. It was an experience, a face, I would never forget.

At every concert, as Truth performed its song "God Is in Control," I was given a personal reminder that no matter how out of control my life might have seemed, God always had everything under control. I loved the words of that song. But in Seattle, on the stage of the church where I had spent all my growing-up years, that song became clearer to me than it had ever been. As we sang its powerful lyrics, out in the audience my nine-year-old nephew stood to his feet, all by himself, and with tears streaming down his face, he lifted his eyes toward heaven and claimed that truth as his own. What a privilege to look out there and see the power of the song's words penetrating his tender young heart and mind.

> God is in control, though godless men conspire.
> His will unfolds though mortal men may always
> seem to doubt.
> His ways are higher than our ways,
> So even through the fire, take heart and know
> God is in control.[3]

My young nephew was facing the greatest hardship of his young life. My sister and her husband, his mom and dad, were getting divorced. As he heard that song for the first time, he looked over at my sister and said, "That song's just for me, Mom." Although he was young, his little life felt out of control. He was weak and hurting.

My sister Bethenee recalls her own vivid memory of his outpouring of pain. "His grief was too large for a nine-year-old body to contain," she said. "I was working downstairs and heard an unusual, high-pitched sound, as if from a little animal in pain. I went upstairs to find where it was coming from and discovered my precious son crouched in the corner of the tub, hiding behind the shower curtain. He looked at me in agony and said, 'I miss my daddy. I need my daddy.' I scooped him up and held him for the next two hours as he cried out his abandonment and pain. I reminded him of his favorite song, 'God Is in Control,' and when he thought of it he felt a sense of peace, believing once again that the truth in that song was just for him," she said.

The power of God is not defined by age or circumstance. No matter who you are or what your story is, his strength takes over in your weakness. He will scoop you up in his arms; he will hold you and never let go. He is more than enough. You may be weak and disheartened, but take heart and know that God is in control.

The Real You

Life is so uncertain. Sometimes it seems like everyone and everything conspires to make us afraid. Afraid of speaking up. Afraid of letting go. Afraid of holding on. Afraid of what people will think. Afraid of being less than perfect. But the Bible says, "God did not give us a spirit that makes us afraid but a spirit of power and love and self-control" (2 Timothy 1:7).

In the space on the next page, write your three biggest fears and why they make you feel so afraid. Be as honest as you can be.

Now remind God of what he said through the apostle Paul in 2 Timothy 1:7 (of course he doesn't *need* a reminder, but he loves to hear from us). Ask him to empower you and help you feel his strength within you. Our God is faithful, unchanging, full of grace and power. He is all you need.

> *Don't be confused, don't be afraid. Everything passes.*
> *God does not change. Patience wins every time. And if*
> *you have God, you lack nothing. God alone is enough.*
> —*Teresa of Avila, paraphrased*

Bethany Hamilton: I'm Still Here

Bethany Hamilton was a girl who had it all: she was an accomplished surfer who had much respect in the surfing world—and she was only thirteen! But on Halloween 2003, everything changed. When she was surfing off the coast of Kauai, Hawaii, Bethany was attacked by a fourteen-foot tiger shark.

She survived, but her arm was severed. Many people thought the tragedy would end her lifelong dream of being a professional surfer, but Bethany was undaunted. Instead of giving up, she leaned hard into her faith in Jesus Christ.

Soon after her accident, Bethany got back on her surfboard and took fifth place at the National Surfing Championships. In August 2004, she took first place in the Open Women's Division.

Her perseverance in becoming a champion surfer could be the happy ending to the story of Bethany Hamilton; instead, it is merely the beginning. Bethany's faith has been transformed by the hardships she has endured, and now she wants to share that faith with the world. She has dedicated her life to inspiring people to overcome adversity, no matter how great the obstacle, and the world is paying attention.

"People I don't even know come up to me. I guess they see me as a symbol of courage and inspiration," she said.

Bethany has been featured in countless magazines, news programs, talk shows, and even commercials. She released a book about her story in October 2004, and now a movie about her life is in the works.

With all the overwhelming changes and challenges she has endured during the past two years, Bethany Hamilton still celebrates her passion. "One thing hasn't changed—and that's how I feel when I'm riding a wave. It's like, Here I am. I'm still here. It's still me and my board—in God's ocean!" she says.

chapter six

Me: The Grand Design

*Wonderful, beautiful is what you see
When you look at me.*

As a young girl, I dreamed of being a school-teacher when I grew up. This usually surprises people; just about everyone expects me to proclaim my lifelong ambition of being a singer. Granted, I spent many afternoons on the hearth of the fireplace, hairbrush microphone in hand, belting out a tune with visions of seeing my name up in lights. My ultimate goal, however, was to teach first grade. That particular grade was my choice because of my deep love for Mrs. Kemp, my own first-grade teacher. She always saw the best in her students and encouraged creativity. I loved Mrs. Kemp for that.

Educators are wonderful, and I have always looked up to them, with the exception of Mrs. Daniels, that one poor teacher who had the misfortune of having toilet paper hanging out of the back of her pants after a trip to the restroom one day. I must admit I made fun of her, which wasn't very nice. But otherwise, I looked at all my teachers through innocent, if not idealistic, eyes.

Of all the gifts and advantages teachers have, it was their control of the blackboard that appealed to me the most. I have no idea why I had such an obsession, but I imagined it as the most glorious thing in the world to hold the chalk in my hand and write freely on the blackboard as little minds soaked up my teachings like a sponge.

Of course it is clear that I did not become a schoolteacher. However, I've come to realize I am instructing others in a way I never imagined. There is no roll to be called, no papers to mark, and no one is bringing me an apple, but through my music I have been given a platform, one I will prayerfully use to encourage, enlighten, and enrich. So in reality, I *am* an educator, of sorts.

LEARNING FROM LIFE'S LESSONS

Before anyone can become the teacher, she must be the student. We are all students, really, learning our way through life. Imagine God up there, holding the chalk at that great, heavenly blackboard, listing our learning opportunities: our mistakes, our weaknesses, our shortcomings, our failures, our successes. Our experiences, good and bad, can make us bitter, or they can make us better. We can ignore what he has taught us, or we can soak up his teachings, apply them to our circumstances, and step up to take our turn at the blackboard.

In that moment when I lay curled up on the bathroom floor, I could not have imagined myself being brave enough to ever speak of my pain out loud. It would never have occurred to me that someday my struggle, my story, might be something God could use. I was a wreck, emotionally and physically. I reeked of vomit, I despised myself for the lie I'd been living, and I felt pathetically weak and totally worthless.

Silly me. I had forgotten that God's strength is made

But me he caught—reached all the way from sky to sea; he pulled me out of that ocean of hate, that enemy chaos, the void in which I was drowning. They hit me when I was down, but God stuck by me. He stood me up on a wide-open field; I stood there saved—surprised to be loved! God made my life complete when I placed all the pieces before him. When I got my act together, he gave me a fresh start. (Psalm 18:16–20 MSG)

perfect in weakness. Just as Jesus had waited patiently for the Samaritan woman to come to the well, God had been waiting for me to land on the cold, hard tiles of that bathroom floor. And although I had no idea then that it was about to happen, I would soon be like the woman at the well, heading out to share with others what had happened to me,

What we are is God's gift to us. What we become is our gift to God.

—Eleanor Powell

C. S. Lewis, in his book *The Problem of Pain*, brilliantly surmises that "God whispers to us in our pleasures, speaks to us in our conscience, but shouts in our pains: It is His megaphone to rouse a deaf world." God is the Great Instructor, and we are his pupils; we learn best through our pain—if only because that's what slows us down enough to make us think.

We all have something we are good at. It may take some of us longer to discover it, and someone else's talent may seem more exciting than ours, but we are all gifted in one way or another. Sometimes it is not in the obvious where we find our destiny. Sometimes God chooses the unlikely, the obscure, the thing we least expect, to reveal his strength and ultimate purpose for us.

Take Big Steps, and Hang On Tight

It's a decision most kids would rather not have to make. Who will you live with when your parents split up? For Grace, seventeen, a brown-eyed pixie with large dimples, the decision was made for her when she was six years old: she would live with her mom until the eighth grade, then she could choose for herself. At the beginning of her ninth-grade year she moved one state north to live with her dad and stepmom, a decision fueled largely by spiritual need. "Though I didn't realize it at the time," she reflects, "I now believe that I moved to my dad's so I could grow as a Christian and be around people who would nurture and encourage that. Before, I was in an environment where what I believed wasn't shared by anyone at school or at home."

Though Grace and her mom didn't share the same views about God, they had a close relationship, and Grace's decision to move away was hard on both of them.

"Something I can say about moving away from my mom is that I wasn't really emotionally ready to do it,' she says matter-of-factly. "It was something I did out of necessity. I don't think that as a fourteen-year-old I was ready to leave my mom. And I don't think that, as a parent, she was ready for me to go. Those first two years were really hard between us. It was almost like moving to college or something, and I didn't realize it was going to be that way until I was already gone. My mom and I shared a whole lot more before I moved to my dad's, and I feel like I'm just now starting to get some of that back."

Grace says that though the move completely rearranged her life and her relationships, she has no regrets about her decision. She believes her need to grow and survive as a Christian somewhat made the choice for her. "You do something because you have to," she explains, "and when you're young, you aren't necessarily able to think through the consequences of that in advance. You can't always be on this spiritual high where everything's great and you understand exactly what God's doing. In the hard times I think it's important to just hang on to faith and hope, and then constantly remind yourself of why you're doing what you're doing."

Jesus, a Friend Like No Other

I began to discover the real me, not through my talents and successes, but when I started embracing my weaknesses and realized I don't have to hold it all together. I *can't* hold it all together. I don't have to have it all figured out. If I did, I would have no need for God. And I sensed that somewhere, wrapped up in the deep recesses of my pain, there was a purpose. I was ready to discover it.

No more hiding. No more running. No more clenching. I had finally let go.

My concept of Jesus was so big that it lacked the personal; instead of focusing on a close connection with him, I had worked long and hard on those relationships I could manipulate through my "Look at me, aren't I great!" mentality. That is why bulimia seemed like such a good option for me for so long—because I believed bulimia kept me thin, and I thought people accepted me more readily when I looked a certain way.

I cannot begin to explain how freeing it was when I embraced Christ as my real Friend. For so long he was simply a gigantic *idea* to me. Although I believed them to be true, the unfathomable images of Savior, Redeemer, and the ultimate sacrifice for mankind made God so big in my mind that what I knew of him didn't translate to what was going on in my everyday life. I had always been told of God's great love, and somewhere inside I believed it. But what completely melted my heart, what completely liberated me from choking insecurity, wasn't just the truth that Jesus loved me but that Jesus *liked* me.

He LIKED me! Exactly as I was. I didn't have to pretend; I didn't have to be a certain size or wear the right jeans. I could be having a bad-hair day, and he would still like me.

It wasn't just my obedience and righteousness he was interested in. He was interested in me. He autographed me on his hand, not because I was born into a great family or because of any of my successes or my attempts at being "cool" or even because he loves me, but because he likes me (see Isaiah 49:16)—"as is."

Here's one way to look at it. I'm a girl who likes to go to the mall. OK, I *love* to go to the mall. I go to the mall a lot. I love a good bargain, but I'm not typically the type who scours the sale racks trying to find the perfect buy. I don't have the patience for that. There are times, however, when the ideal item crosses my path. I instantly fall in love with it . . . but then I see there's something wrong with it—a missing button, a broken zipper, or a seam that's starting to come apart. But usually when I find those flaws, I'm happy, not sad, because that's an instant discount, one I'm all too happy to take advantage of. So I purchase the item, get my discount, and say, "Thank you very much." Often the salesperson writes on the tag, "Sold as is, no return."

That is how Jesus accepts us: AS IS. Broken, cracked, tattered, and in all of our ordinariness, he receives us with a no-return policy. He never gives up on us, and he will never give us back. That is a friend in the truest sense of the word. He looks at me, with my freckles, my large pores, and my even larger sins, and says, "You are wonderfully and beautifully made."

Jesus had long been my Redeemer, but when I accepted Jesus as my real Friend and began *living* like he was my Friend, my true healing began. I was ready to discover the truth of who I am without the masks, without the pretenses, without the charade. Knowing and understanding Jesus as my Friend helped me see myself in a new light; the security I found in my relationship with him helped me open the door of possibility and see a glimpse of the person I could be.

The Turning Point

Now, I want to stress that the healing of your self-image, and any destructive behavior linked to it, may occur differently than mine did. I was fortunate to find exactly what I needed through prayer, reflection, and studying God's Word along with other resources. I hope the story I share here and in the next few chapters will inspire you and encourage you to discover the real you, the person God created you to be. But I know it's also possible that you may need additional help, and if you do please don't hesitate to seek it out. Christian therapists have been a godsend to many people who are struggling with self-esteem issues and the problems they cause, and Christian organizations such as Remuda Ranch help clients follow a godly path toward recovery from eating disorders.

In the back of the book I've listed some of the organizations as well as publications I found invaluable as I worked, with God's help, to become the girl he sees. I hope they're helpful to you in your own journey toward healing.

For me, the turning point was feeling Jesus's comforting presence around me on the bathroom floor. Jesus: a Friend like no other. Amazingly, he accepts me—truly accepts me—just as I am.

For me, the turning point was feeling Jesus's comforting presence around me on the bathroom floor. *Jesus: a Friend like no other.* Amazingly, he accepts me—truly accepts me—just as I am. When that truth finally penetrated my brain, I felt authenticated for the first time in my life. I had been an actress for so long, wearing my masks of success, happiness, strength, and pride while in truth I was being held prisoner by the disease of bulimia, making myself throw up repeatedly throughout each day. The world thought I had it made; Jesus knew I was living in misery. When I understood that he liked me despite my destructive behavior—and that he would continue to like me now and for always, honestly and unconditionally—I felt real hope at last. My Savior was also my Friend. Unconditionally.

Once I accepted that Jesus loved me in my "as-is" condition, to continue trying to be anyone or anything but my true self felt beyond dishonest. Instead of being the me I had invented, I was now free to be the *real* me. And once I accepted that Jesus not only loves but *likes* the real me, I realized others might feel the same way.

I was finally ready to begin living, really living. But how do you suddenly go from being plastic to being real? I wasn't sure. But that was OK. I didn't have to have all the answers.

I would be lying if I said I that one day I just decided to stop throwing up, stop starving myself, and start believing in *me*. It wasn't quite that simple. There were many days when I fell back into my old habits. Many times I felt ugly and insecure. However, slowly but surely, one step at a time, I was seeing myself differently.

There is a reason the Bible tells us to set our minds on "things which are above" (Colossians 3:1 KJV). I began to think about, truly dwell on, the promises of God. As I read and soaked up everything I could that would remind me of my value to God, slowly but surely I began to believe in his promises—and believe in *me*.

God was giving me new eyes.

REAL GIRL, REAL LIFE

The Great In-Between

There's a pretty fine line between little girl and blossoming young woman. One still likes to climb trees; the other has a full-time job. One still plays with Barbie dolls (even if it's in secret); the other memorizes the quadratic formula and prepares to tackle college entrance exams. Angel, sixteen, is both: a bubbly junior in high school and the poster child for those preparing to make the perilous leap from adolescence to adulthood.

"I think one of the hardest things about being a teenager today is being sort of in-between," she says. "A lot of teenagers are stressed out by the tasks of everyday living— homework, deadlines, work, relationships. And while I definitely have my moments with those things, I'd have to say that I'm more worried about my future than what's going on today. These days there's so much pressure to plan your future; you have to make good grades so you can go to college. You have to go to college so you can have this great career. Everything we're doing now seems to be about planning for the future. But what about today?

"I have nothing against Advanced Placement classes," she continues. "I'm in one. But there's this subtle message of, *Take care of some college while you're in high school so you can get a good job sooner! Don't get left behind; get more done faster!* I understand it on one level, but I think on another level it robs kids of their childhood. In many ways they're treating us like we're already college students. I know it's wise to prepare for the college years, but I think there's definitely something to be said for enjoying the end of your childhood while you're still in high school!"

In a perfect world, Angel says, childhood wouldn't be a competition, a race, or a contest of survival of the fittest. It would be OK to slow down, to not have the right answers, to just be. And to let God do the prep work.

Mysterious Ways and Wonders

God's timing is always perfect. My parents always had pretty good timing too. That sense of timing was apparent the first time they told me I had been "prophesied" over. Now, I have to admit, the whole *prophesy* thing conjured up images in my mind of sweaty television evangelists and their fainting followers. But at the same time, I knew that all of us have a special, God-given destiny, and he has his way of revealing that destiny to each of us in a very personal and individual way. He moves as he sees fit, and I believed what my parents told me about the prophecy they had been given for me.

Around the time I was conceived, my father's job kept him away from home quite a bit during the week; to my mom it seemed as though he traveled half the year. She had her hands full being a full-time, stay-at-home mother of four. She loved it and has always said she wouldn't change a moment of it, but she had her fair share of pull-her-hair-out moments.

Turns out I was an unexpected pregnancy. After all, Mom and Dad already had four children and were not planning on more. So when Mom found out she was pregnant, she felt overwhelmed, inadequate to handle so much. Dad, I'm sure, was just as surprised as she was.

My parents had not shared the news with anyone, not even family. Then came that Sunday when they went to the church where my mom taught second-grade Sunday school. While they were there, Mrs. Nelson, a sweet lady in the church but not necessarily a close friend of Mom's, pulled her aside and whispered these words into her ear: *"The child you are carrying will be a great joy to you and to the church."*

My mom, shocked by the unexpected message, stood amazed at the power of God. Shocked, amazed—and comforted. God saw her. Not in some big, general God-sees-all-of-humanity sort of a way, but in a deeply personal way. He cared enough to send her a voice-mail message, and although it wasn't his voice she heard, she knew he had sent the messenger.

Amazingly, my parents didn't tell me this story until I was older—after I had moved to Nashville and gotten my first record deal. Why? They never wanted me to feel the pressure of living up to that remarkable prophecy. Instead, they had decided to trust God and simply watch it unfold.

Looking back, I see that in addition to the prophecy, they also had been given divine wisdom—and that good timing I mentioned—in a way they couldn't have known. This wisdom guided them in waiting to tell me about the message, and when they did tell me, they did so hoping to provide peace and assurance to me as I stepped out in faith with my new music career. And they did. But it was so much more than that. What they didn't know was, they were telling me at the height of my bulimia.

The story that had provided comfort to my mom at such a weak moment was now doing the same for me. *He sees me,* I thought to myself. *And he has made me special. I am unique. I am set apart.*

Finally understanding that Jesus loves me—and better yet, likes me—I gradually began liking myself. And I became convinced that God sees me. God cares about me. God knows me. You may not discover this truth in such a dramatic, unusual way as I did, but that doesn't make it any less true. God whispers his love for us in the wind; he clears a path for us through the thickest forest, even though we never recognize that it's his hand clearing the debris out of our way. He knows our insecurities and our deepest desires, and he's given every one of us a dream. Whether we feel inadequate, ill equipped, ordinary, or "un-special," he has created us for this journey toward our own individual destiny, and he is with us every step of the way.

GETTING REAL WITH GOD: DAD'S DELIGHT

From Our Abba Father, We Get What We Don't Deserve

> The LORD your God is with you; the mighty One will save you. He will rejoice over you. You will rest in his love; he will sing and be joyful about you. (Zephaniah 3:17)

There's something almost magical about the story told in Luke 15:11–24, best known as Jesus's parable of the prodigal son. Certainly it's a story we can all relate to. The younger of two sons grows tired of life on the farm. He's heard about all the fun and entertainment the world has to offer, and he wants to experience some of that for himself. After all, he's young, and he deserves a little fun, right? So he pesters his dad to let him cash out his inheritance early, and although his dad knows the trouble his son is asking for, he caves in and gives him the money. And off the son goes to live life on his own terms.

Months later, when the money runs out and his party friends desert him, the son finds himself living in squalor, starving and miserable.

If you ask me, this is the point where the real story actually cranks up. The dad knew his son was making a mistake but loved him enough to let him go. Then, day after day, month after month, he looked down the driveway out to the main road, hoping his kid would come home. No doubt he asked God to bring his son back safely.

When that day finally came, as the son dragged his raggedy, malnourished self back up the path he'd known all his life, his dad saw him in the distance. And in his mercy, with unconditional acceptance and love, the dad ran to meet him. He didn't wait for his son to knock on the door or approach him as he waited in the yard. He ran to meet him, saying, "Give my boy the best clothes we've got, throw some steaks on the grill, and get ready to celebrate because my son was lost and now is found!" He didn't say, "I told you so," or "Well, you got what you deserved, kid!" No, the dad freely forgave his son and felt great joy at his return.

The story of the prodigal son, you see, is not so much about the son and his frailties and stupid mistakes as it is about the kind of father he had. He had the kind of dad who never gives up and never lets go, and most of all, delights and takes great pride and joy in his child.

Some of us are blessed to have such a dad in our lives, but many can't imagine what that kind of real-life dad would be like. The thing is, that's the kind of Father our God is. Abba Father is the kind of Dad who knows us better than we know ourselves and loves us even more. He's the kind of Dad who will let us go but longs for our return—the kind of Dad who sings songs of joy over us and who loves us unconditionally, even when we don't deserve it.

Even when we forget how much we mean to him and how much we need him.

The Real You

In the space on the next page, write the name of a person you absolutely *love* to be around, a person who makes everything brighter and fun, full of life and laughter. A person who makes you feel good about yourself, who brings out the best in you.

How does it feel to know that God feels the same way about you? That he delights in you and rejoices over you and thinks you're wonderful . . . just as you are?

Kim Meeder: Brokeness, Like Stained Glass . . .

Nine-year-old Kim Meeder climbed awkwardly onto the little mare, anxiety swirling in her heavy heart. She'd never been on a horse before, but something in the horse's eyes, in the way the mare responded to her touch, told her Kim was safe . . . and loved . . . and that everything would be OK.

How she needed to believe those things on that day, of all days!

It was the day her parents were buried. Her father, unable to face the bitter divorce ahead, had killed his wife and then committed suicide. Their deaths shattered Kim's already shaky world. But that day, riding as fast as she dared, Kim galloped out to the edge of her childhood and into the arms of a loving God.

Looking back, Kim Meeder, now forty-two, understands how that day was a turning point in her life. "That was the first day I understood unconditional love of the Lord through a horse," she says. "And how ironic and completely not coincidental that my personal tragedy was the beginning of what we're doing here now."

Today, Kim and her husband, Troy, own and operate Crystal Peaks Youth Ranch, a nine-acre plot of heaven on earth for neglected, abused horses and broken, neglected children. It's a humble piece of red crust in the Cascade Mountains of central Oregon where in only nine years, more than three hundred horses have been rescued and more than twenty-five thousand children have found hope and healing.

When Kim and Troy cashed in their life savings to buy the land, they knew it would take years of grit and determination to restore it. "But isn't it just like the Lord to choose the broken and useless things in this world to show his greatest glory?" Kim asks, not for an answer, but as the answer. "In our brokenness, he begins to fit everything back together . . . like stained glass that is beautiful beyond words."

Miracles occur almost daily at Crystal Peaks. A five-year-old boy who has suffered terrible abuse at the hands of his own father reaches out for the love offered by a once-battered horse. A young girl, devastated by constant ridicule at school, finds unconditional acceptance and a horse dream of her own. A rescued horse gives a dying man his last wish. Here, physical pain is momentarily relieved in the calming freedom found in the company of these gentle animals. Emotionally starved, rejected children feel loved and chosen for the first time in their lives. These everyday miracles are undoubtedly God's way of reminding Kim and Troy that nothing is beyond his reach.

"One of the foundational verses of my life is 2 Corinthians 1:3–4," Kim says. "'All praise to the God and Father of our Lord Jesus Christ. He is the source of every mercy and the God who comforts us. He comforts us in our troubles so that we can comfort others. When others are troubled, we will be able to give them the same comfort God has given us' (NLV). These verses assure me that suffering has a purpose and that a tragic event can become a healing event, not only in your life, but in the lives of all the people God brings you in contact with.

"And so, in my mind, every time I have the opportunity to touch the hearts of children with what I've been through, that heals me. It's the power of Christ within us. There's victory through tragedy. And these big, raking scars in our hearts—instead of being raw, open wounds—become beauty marks for God's glory."

chapter seven

Beautiful Lies

You're turning the tattered
fabric of my life
Into a perfect tapestry.

he current state of my life finds me in way too many airports, flying from city to city as I live out my musical dream. More than half the month, I'm in a different place every day, juggling radio interviews, running through sound checks, performing in concerts, doing backstage meet-and-greets, and trying to fit in time for my personal life.

Sometimes things get crazy, but I feel remarkably blessed to wake up every day and do what I love. To think that what I would be doing as a favorite hobby has instead become my profession is like living a dream come true. It's almost like being given the keys to the mall and told, "Pick out everything you want, and we'll not only pay for it but we'll pay *you* to wear it."

But, as I've mentioned, there *are* some things that make a music career a bit challenging, at times. For instance, I have a major fear of flying. But when I'm in Charlotte, North Carolina, one day and I have to be in Sacramento, California, the next, a plane is pretty much my only option. Alas, I spend way too much money on the 2/$1.99 bags of peanuts and those dreaded fashion and gossip magazines. I know I shouldn't read them. I know I shouldn't let those images fill my mind, but when I am walking by the news-stand, it's as if the headlines jump off the page, wrap themselves around my throat, and strangle me until I give in. So there I sit in the gate area, nervously waiting to board a plane I don't want to be on, eating stale, over-priced peanuts, and looking at beauty I will never attain. At least two of the three of those activities are definitely not part of the treatment plan for someone try to improve her self-image!

THE DECEPTIVE PROMISES OF "BEAUTY"

One day, thinking of beauty, I decided to play a word-association game. I wrote down the first five things that came to my mind when I thought of the word *beautiful*:

1. long legs
2. tiny waist
3. flawless skin
4. toned all over
5. laughter

OK, what is wrong with this picture?

I had a warped view of beauty, that's what! Only one of those things really belonged on that list. Laughter really *is* beautiful. It's wonderful, a balm for the broken spirit. But what about those other things? Why were physical attributes the things I thought of first (not to mention, they were physical attributes I feel I don't have)?

The Mark of Beauty

What about you? When you hear the word *beautiful,* what do you think of? Write down the first five words that come to mind.

1.

2.

3.

4.

5.

From where or from whom did you get your understanding of beauty?

Pop culture's beauty mark has been stamped into our brains, and it's a very narrow definition of *beauty*. The media would lead us to believe that beauty and physical attractiveness are synonymous and that with the right clothes and makeup, the right body, we can live happily ever after. Truth is, the airbrushed images they set forth are largely impossible to attain.

Reality television would lead us to believe that whatever we don't like about ourselves we can fix with cosmetic surgery and that once we get the surgery, our life will be magically harmonious and perfect. In movies, magazines, television, and music, we are constantly fed the lie that pretty people always finish first. But then contradictory headlines reveal that yet another Hollywood star has fallen victim to an eating disorder or to drug addiction or even to suicide. We read the story and think, *How could this happen? She has everything anyone could want: success, beauty, wealth, fame, security.*

It happens because none of those things matter when she lays her head on her pillow at night. She feels empty and worthless.

So many of us have our sense of legitimacy and respect wrapped up in what the world says is beautiful. We have fallen for the lie that beauty is about how we look on the outside instead of who we are on the inside. The dominant standards of body weight and shape, illustrated by the abnormally underweight models on TV and in movies and magazines, continue to emphasize the idea that thin is beautiful. Maybe that is why the National Eating Disorders Association cites research that in North America up to ten million girls and women and one million boys and men suffer from an eating disorder (see nationaleatingdisorders.org; click on "eating disorders info" then "statistics"). Because of the guilt and secretiveness of the condition, many cases go unreported, so it is likely that accurate numbers are much higher.

Researchers also uncovered the fact that 42 percent of first- through third-grade girls want to be thinner. What happened to innocence? Six- and seven-year-old girls are supposed to be worried about running away from "yucky" boys, playing with dolls, and figuring out their favorite ice-cream flavor. Instead, they are looking to their mirrors as a measuring stick for self-worth. Even at such a tender age, they're desperate to hear the words "I love you just as you are."

REAL GIRL, REAL LIFE

Underneath the Swan

You can spot her a mile away by her hair. The long, red nest of curls is the envy of some and the quandary of others. "Anna's hair is going to be a problem," says one drill team director to another as the girls polish a dance for competition. There's a smattering of laughter, then one teammate suggests that Anna cut it.

"That made me so mad," confesses Anna, "because she's implying that I should change who I am to conform to a standard of uniformity. And I'm not going to do that."

It's not always been easy for this classical music–loving, Sponge Bob–watching, sixteen-year-old to accept who she is. In middle school she went on an extended fast to fit into "skinny jeans," and she often bought clothes with an eye for what she thought others would like rather than what appealed to her. Over the years, however, Anna says the school of hard knocks has taught her a lesson or two about the high price of popularity.

"If I could go back and talk to myself when I was twelve years old," she reflects, "I would tell myself not to bother keeping up with trends, because they change so quickly. I could go out right now and buy all the stylish clothes, but three months from now I might look back and say, 'What was I thinking?' It's pretty much impossible to keep up with all these trends and fashions and look good on the outside without trying too hard on the inside to be something you're not. A lot of times some of the most graceful, beautiful people are like a swan or duck on the lake. They may look like they're gliding along, but underneath they're paddling like crazy. You may see a drop-dead-gorgeous teenager walking down the hall with perfect hair and makeup, but what you don't see is that she spent an hour fighting with her hair in the morning and has skipped lots of meals to be able to fit into a certain outfit. In my opinion, the lengths to which some people go to 'measure up' are not at all worth the effort. It's so much easier to just be who you *are*."

Jumping off the fashion-go-round, Anna says, is easier said than done, but if you truly believe that beauty is more than skin deep, you'll want to take a closer look at what you're made of, what you are on the inside. Take an inventory of the real you.

"I'm not perfect," Anna says, "but I'm an original. I'm smart. I'm kind. I'm strong. If people like me, great, but if they don't, it doesn't change who I am. And the real kicker is, when you know what's real on the inside, the stress of measuring up on the inside just isn't an issue."

The Beauty Blitz

My niece is a smart, beautiful eight-year-old with fiery red hair and a dynamic personality to match. She has been so fun to watch, always footloose and fancy free, fluttering through her days like a little butterfly. I love her free spirit. But I became troubled when I noticed her growing preoccupation with her body shape and fashion sense. While I was visiting at Christmastime, she confided to me that she doesn't feel as pretty as her classmates and that she views herself as chubby.

Chubby! She's only eight years old!

I wrapped my arms around her and tried my best to convince her how special and unique she is—how truly beautiful she is, inside and out—while fearing that the overwhelming voice of the media may drown out mine. Thankfully she has two parents who are also working on a daily basis to instill in her mind her true value. But the reality still remains that even with an ideal upbringing, it's very likely she will struggle with her self-image.

That was, after all, the situation I had grown up in. I had an ideal upbringing. I did not come from a broken home. I was in a positive, loving environment, and my parents continually showed me how much they believed in me. Yet I was full of insecurity and self-doubt.

So how could it happen? I don't really know, but I suspect that the influence of my peers and of modern culture somehow eclipsed the positive things my parents and family were showering upon me. Maybe the same thing happened to you.

Summing it all up, friends, I'd say you'll do best by filling your minds and meditating on things true, noble, reputable, authentic, compelling, gracious—the best, not the worst; the beautiful, not the ugly; things to praise, not things to curse. Put into practice what you learned from me, what you heard and saw and realized. Do that, and God, who makes everything work together, will work you into his most excellent harmonies. (Philippians 4:8–9 MSG)

Blitzed by the media, we are continually bombarded with voices and images that seem to dictate what we ought to look like. Problem is, in real life most fashion models don't look anything like their magazine pictures. Toned by their personal trainer, tanned by a spray, sculpted by a cosmetic surgeon, hair-styled by the best professionals, makeup painted on by someone using the greatest products available, illuminated by ideal lighting—and all of this captured by a world-class photographer. I've already shared how I experienced some of these procedures firsthand. After hundreds of shots, the editors pick the best one, and if it is still not perfect, the model is digitally enhanced through a computer. No wonder our perception of reality is so far off and our thoughts are so consumed with our physical appearance!

Given how pervasive the focus on outward beauty is in our culture, I guess it was silly of me to think I might grow out of the whole faulty-self-image, need-for-perfection thing. Judging by all the "mature" Hollywood stars and other celebrities who are lining up for face-lifts, accepting ourselves for who we are on the inside apparently doesn't come more easily as we age. Although some of the peer-pressure issues of youth fall away, new pressures take their place. Growing expectations come into play. And the aging process fights us every step of the way.

These days more and more people are tempted to follow the celebrities' lead and seek out plastic surgery to fix whatever they don't like about their physical appearance. Cosmetic surgery is not just on the rise; it has skyrocketed as our culture becomes more and more obsessed with perfection.

I read a letter from a woman not long ago who had gone "under the knife" *twenty-six* times. Twenty-six different plastic surgeries! With every surgery she said she noticed something else, something more that needed just a little fixing. She said that until she looks in the mirror and sees perfection, she will not be satisfied.

The truth is, she will never find satisfaction in her mirror, no matter how many surgeries she has. Satisfaction will come only when she "operates" on that unique person who lives beneath her outer shell.

REAL GIRL, REAL LIFE

"I Gotta Be Me"

With bottle-blonde hair, super-thick black mascara, and an apple tattoo on her ankle, Amanda seems older than eighteen. Maybe it's because she practically raised her little

But why are people important to you? Why do you take care of human beings? You made them a little lower than the angels and crowned them with glory and honor.
(Psalm 8:4–5)

brother and sister while her mom worked two jobs. Or maybe it's because she drives a not-so-cool clunker of a car now that she's a college freshman.

No, it's more than that. Amanda really gets the trouble with "growing up girl." In fact, she "got it" early.

"My first year in high school was horrible," she says. "I didn't just change schools. My whole life was changing. We were really struggling at home, but I was determined to do whatever it took to fit in. I tried to wear the right clothes, tried to be thin enough, tried not to say the wrong things. But trying to be one of the 'in' people was exhausting.

"I just remember, one day at my locker, looking around and seeing this whole pack of girls wearing basically the same clothes, the same hairstyle, the same makeup, carrying the same bags, and wearing the same brands. They all walked the same way and spent most of their time hitting on the boys, and I thought, *Is that all you're worth? You're trying so hard to fit in, you might as well be clones! So much for being true to yourself!*"

Amanda hadn't grown up in church, but she knew enough about God to know that he made her for more than that kind of life. "I was so grossed out by that whole scene, that's when I stopped caring about what they thought of me."

Distancing herself from the pack made for a lonely senior year. It was as if the "in" girls overheard her unspoken decision and felt determined to make her pay. "Where'd you get that skirt, Kmart?" was about the kindest thing they had to say.

But Amanda learned to value a witty comeback: "Actually, it's a Tar-zshay [Target] original" delivered with a quizzical smile. And better still, she began to value the realness and honesty of "the uncool." She made it her mission to not only find it but to encourage it in others. "You think there are a lot of fakers out there, and there are," she says, "but there are a lot of beautiful, real, and true people too. You just have to look."

Life is still tough at times. It probably always will be for outsiders, says Amanda. But her bright eyes and bigger-than-life smile tell you all you need to know. And if that isn't enough, her T-shirt backs it up: "I gotta be me."

Taking Back What's True

If all we do is look at our outer shell, we're not all that unique. For example, there are many people who look like me: blonde, medium-length hair; petite; blue eyes. Actually, I think I have really pretty eyes. They are as blue as the Caribbean Sea. The depth of their color reminds me of the true depth that is inside me.

Writing that felt funny, but it also felt good. Why are we so timid to point out the things we like about ourselves? I've always spent my time listing those things about me that I *don't* like. But it sure feels good to recognize those things about my shell that I do like.

But who I am isn't the color of my eyes. I am the one peering out of them. I am the one who is hiding inside this skin of mine. And who is that, exactly? Well, I'm still figuring that out. I don't know if there is one answer or several. I am not the woman I was five years ago, and hopefully I am not the woman I will be five years from now. I am evolving, changing, becoming. Maybe it's not so much who I am but that I am a work in progress, striving to become more like the One who made me.

I have not intended this book to be an infomercial on how to be happy with your looks and get the life you've always wanted. Jesus is not a genie in a bottle; we don't get three wishes for a perfect life. Sooner or later everyone experiences

So as it turns out, we do not have a little tame domestic God, thank God, but we do have a huge, wild, dangerous God—dangerous of course only if we think that God ought to be manageable and safe; a God of almost manic creativity, ingenuity and enthusiasm; a Big-Enough God, who is also a supremely generous and patient God; a God of beauty and chance and solidarity.[1]

—Sara Maitland

the reality that sometimes life is hard, pain is tangible, and hurt is genuine. But Jesus, who looks past the shell to the you inside, is interested in the details.

We all know people who constantly look at everything but us while we're talking to them, distracted instead of listening. Not Jesus. In fact, I believe if he were physically sitting in the room with me he would stop to hear my story, and while he listened, he would look me in the eye.

Maybe it makes you a little uncomfortable to picture yourself sitting alone with Jesus in a personal get-acquainted session. Maybe you're like me—or at least like the me I used to be and try hard *not* to be now. If so, you sometimes feel inadequate, illegitimate, inferior, and imperfect, even though you've been told again and again that those aren't the feelings you were created to have. Maybe you know who Jesus is, but you don't *know* him. You have prayed until you are out of breath, yet you still feel empty and incomplete, so you stopped praying.

Try again. Talk to him. Ask him to become evident to you. And once you've asked him to authenticate himself, you must also be genuine with him. You have to be real.

The Real You

Your self-image is not this ethereal, theoretical thing that is hard to get your hands around. It is who and what you picture yourself to be. How you feel about *you*. Do you base how you feel about yourself on the expectations of others? On whether you have the right clothes, live in the right neighborhood, belong with the popular people? If so, your self-image isn't a true reflection of who you really are. Every girl has a vision of who she is. Who do you think *you* are?

True self-worth is not based on what you feel about yourself or even on what others think about you. True self-esteem can only be based on how God sees you. You are only who God says you are.

And God says you are wonderful.

To be real, you have to take back your mind, snatching it away from the powerful influence of the media images you see everywhere. You have to see yourself as God sees you.

And what exactly *does* he see when he looks at us?

God's definition of beauty is vastly different from the world's standard, so it may be easier to answer that question by first saying what he *doesn't* see. He doesn't see a flawed failure. Remember, he doesn't make mistakes. He sees us as beautiful, and if we then view ourselves as anything less, it's like we're saying to God, "Hey, maybe you need to get your eyes checked."

You are not a flawed creature, an accident in God's otherwise-perfect design. You are the beautiful handiwork of God, and he has a plan and a purpose for your life. Now, I know it's one thing to *say* those words, but it's another to believe them and live out, isn't it?

For me, it begins by putting down those magazines of lies and picking up the Book of Truth. As I have immersed myself in the Bible, I've learned that I am who God says I am. According to the psalmist, God "made me in an amazing and wonderful way" (139:14). Who am I to question the craftsmanship of the Creator of the universe?

So what is the beauty we *should* pursue? First Peter 3:3–4 tells us, "It is not fancy hair, gold jewelry, or fine clothes that should make you beautiful. No, your beauty

Best be yourself, imperial, plain and true!

—Elizabeth Barrett Browning

should come from within you—the beauty of a gentle and quiet spirit that will never be destroyed and is very precious to God."

I tried for so long to be perfect. I wanted so badly to look like those girls in my magazines that I harmed my health trying to find validation. But finally I found that the greatest sense of self came from finding my worth in God.

I'm not saying I no longer care how I look. I still love fashion. I find great satisfaction in adapting the latest trends to my personal style and wearing them modestly. I am always trying to find a new way to motivate myself to exercise, and I remind myself that taking care of my health is respecting the body God gave me. I love lip gloss, and I'm always looking for a new method to achieve that rosy complexion, so far be it from me to tell anyone not to wear makeup! But I've learned that if I want to have a true glow, I have to fix my focus on God, not on my makeup case. The Bible says, "Those who look to him are radiant" (Psalm 34:5 NIV). We become more attractive by cultivating our inner beauty.

As I looked to God, I found the key to my self-worth. As I uncovered the truth of what Jesus really thinks about me, how he loves and accepts me, I was finally able to begin accepting myself. I discovered my sense of being. In short, when I found the real Jesus, I finally discovered the real me. That's when I became the girl God sees.

GETTING REAL WITH GOD: THE ONE WHO KNOWS YOU BEST AND LOVES YOU MOST

The Joy of Knowing God Chooses Each of Us First

The Lord spoke his word to me, saying: "Before I made you in your mother's womb, I chose you." (Jeremiah 1:4–5)

Nothing good ever happened at recess. So Danielle, a sweet, precocious third grader, did her best to get out of it. She'd volunteer to help clean up the classroom, or she'd let the teacher know she wasn't feeling well enough to go out and play. She'd do almost anything to avoid going outside—especially in the spring, because that was when team sports ruled recess. And that meant the absolute most unbearable thing about being Danielle, the girl nobody wanted on the team.

But on those horrible days when team sports were unavoidable, she'd stand among her classmates, her eyes to the ground, as back and forth the team captains would say, "I'll take Billy," "I'll take Jessica," "I'll take Jason." One by one the little crowd of students would walk away to stand beside the one who chose them. One by one, they'd high-five each other and shout, "Yeah!" when certain kids were chosen. But there was never a "Yeah!" for Danielle. Inevitably, she was the last kid left standing there, all alone.

And as if that weren't bad enough, then the worst would happen: "Who's gonna take Danielle?" one of the kids would ask the team captains. By then they were usually walking away, eager to get the game started.

"You take her," one would say.

"No, you take her," would come the reply.

Eventually, during a ritual that seemed to take hours, Danielle would be assigned (she was never really "chosen"); then she would shuffle over and stand with the team who had taken her but didn't want her to play the game she didn't want to play.

Danielle's story is shared by thousands, maybe millions, of kids all over the world. The fat kids. The poor kids. The slow kids. The disabled kids. The bullied kids. The throwaway kids. The angry kids. Kids who are dying on the inside. Imagine how revolutionary it would be if all the outcasts who ever stood on that field waiting to be chosen were not only wanted, but chosen first! Can you imagine? Being chosen first, being wanted, could change their lives forever.

In the opening verses of the book of Jeremiah, God makes one thing exceptionally clear: before he made us in our mother's womb (which in itself was quite intentional on his part), he chose us. He tells Jeremiah that he is set apart for a special work, appointed as a prophet to the nations. You and I may not be prophets like Jeremiah was, but the truth of what God said to him is also for us today.

We are *chosen*. We are set apart. We are meant to live big, big lives full of joy—unafraid, loved supremely by the

One who created us. And God didn't choose us because he thinks we're always going to win. In fact, he chose us knowing that we may be clumsy, self-conscious, ashamed, too quick to give our opinion, dreadful at listening, full of pride, shy, too smart for our own good, or possessing a host of other characteristics that are deemed by the world as the traits of a loser. God knows us intimately, in all our imperfections, and he loves us beyond measure. That truth won't make the playground any less cruel for the Danielles in the world, but that truth—rooted deeply in our hearts, coloring every thought that runs through our minds—is more than enough to see us through the game.

The Real You

When was the last time you were eagerly chosen, picked out of the crowd, or given recognition? Do you remember what that felt like? Were you surprised, or did you see it coming? How did the people around you react? What would your life look like today if you truly believed what God says about you in Jeremiah 1:4–5?

Make this your prayer today and every day:

"Lord, thank you for loving me just as I am. When I start to believe what the world says about me, when I begin to allow the negative thoughts to consume my mind, remind me you don't believe that nonsense. You believe in me. It doesn't matter to you what kind of family I come from or how much money I have or whether I can walk and chew gum at the same time. You think I'm amazing! Help me see myself as you see me, to believe the truth you spoke to Jeremiah, and to love the person you made me to be."

Just Like You: Young Women Who Touched the World

Nicole Mullen: Beyond the Music

To look at her now—a beautiful, vivacious mother of three with a successful marriage and celebrated music career—it's hard to imagine anything less than perfect. But Nicole Mullen would be the first to tell you that perfection is neither her goal nor the reality. Being real is.

Growing up in Cincinnati, Nicole was blessed with godly parents who loved and adored her. But the outside world was cruel. "I wasn't cute, and I didn't have a lot of stuff. Along with my store-bought things, a lady from church would make clothes for me and my sisters," she says. "Some girls on the school bus would make fun of us. Every morning, without fail I would hear, 'Here comes homemade!' But I remember thinking, God still has a plan for me that these girls cannot touch. And I came to the conclusion that it really wasn't up to them to determine how I was going to turn out. It was up to God and me. The choice was mine."

This "ugly duckling" always knew she wanted to be a singer, and she received little encouragement. Even so, she started writing her own songs at age twelve, mostly to work through her feelings of self-doubt and insecurity. Her high school counselor told her she'd never make a living at it. But she kept on singing and writing every chance she got.

After high school, she began with a seven-dollar-per-hour job as a studio backup singer, then one thing led to another. Eventually Nicole got a recording contract with an independent music label, followed by a gig as a backup singer with Amy Grant, a job that led to more opportunities. Twenty-plus Dove Award and Grammy Award nominations later—most recently she won the 2005 Dove Award for Female Vocalist of the Year—Nicole is one of the most respected and acclaimed artists in all of Christian music.

But if you ask her, being a singer is not what life's all about. It's just what she does for a living. "Sometimes we think we are what we do," she explains. "We are not. I am not a singer. I sing. That is what I do. But I am Nicole—the mother, the wife, the friend, the daughter, the mentor, the mentee—that's who I am."

So the music career is nothing but a platform for sharing an important message. "My goal in life is to encourage people who are listening," Nicole says. "How can I make the next four minutes of this song worth more than just four minutes? How can I leave somebody with hope? That's my goal, and if I accomplish that, then it's worth more than a Grammy, worth more than a Dove, worth more than any of them," she says.

Working toward that goal, Nicole established an ongoing ministry to young girls, the Baby Girls Club, a ministry of encouragement, mentoring, and relationship. Each Wednesday afternoon, Nicole spends hours with these girls, talking, laughing, doing homework, dancing, singing, and sharing what it means to be a young woman who respects and believes in God first and then herself.

Nicole is one of those incredible women who boldly lives what she believes, without hesitation. "The world is looking for someone who believes in something. What do you believe in? I believe in Christ, and for that I will not apologize. I travel around the country singing to young people, encouraging them to give their lives to Christ while they are young. Live it. Talk it. Christ is real. Without him, I'd have nothing to sing about."

chapter eight

With New Eyes

Beautiful is what you see
When you look at me.

*P*rayer after prayer, tear after tear, day by day, and
moment by moment, the outside matters less.
Sure, I'd like to say it doesn't matter at all, but let's be real:
I still have short legs. I still have freckles. I still have cellulite
in unmentionable places. I'm still fragile. I'm still human.
But it does matter less.

As long as there are mirrors and reflections to be seen in
them, I will notice something about myself I would like to
change. Society's programming and the pressure to live up
to someone else's standard of beauty doesn't magically disappear. But I've learned a valuable secret: I can simply choose

not to look so much. I've spent too much of my life obsessing over this outer shell, so now I just don't give myself a lot of time in front of the mirror to think too much about it.

That, and my eyesight has improved. Once I decided to truly discover Jesus, he gave me new eyes so I could learn to see myself in a different light.

I always knew that finding the real me would be a long and difficult road of self-discovery. But it was easier than I thought it would be because I had the answer all along. That answer was right in front of me. It was behind me. It was beside me. It was inside of me. The answer was and always is *Jesus*.

When you're fighting your way back from something like bulimia, it's important to *tell someone*. Then the whole secret thing loses its luster. I confided in a trusted youth leader who served as both a confidant and a source of accountability for me. I also did research to find helpful books, including books that explained the Scripture to me more clearly.

I'm not trying to oversimplify anything. My pain was real. My affliction was all too obvious, my need all too palpable. There was not some magic formula and then *poof!* everything was suddenly OK. Jesus is the answer, but when we find him, life's problems don't just disappear. Life is a journey, a process.

Unfortunately, and much to my frustration, this fact

causes confusion among many Christians, many churches. All of us struggle, but too often we are afraid to speak of our problems because we've not been given the freedom to be human. *Failure* is a dirty word. We can share glorious testimonies of how God delivered us from this or that, but if we're smack in the middle of the problem, we'd best be quiet about it. We like to wrap up Christianity in a nice package with a pretty little bow on top and hand it out with an imaginary card that reads, "Become a Christian and go to church and you will have a wonderful, perfect life. You'll be just like us!"

Just like us? If we've plastered on the same plastic smiles and false-front happiness as the rest of the world, who would *want* that kind of life?

OK, so that would be me; or rather, that would be the old Natalie. I thought by wearing a happy-face mask I was demonstrating the Christian experience to everyone around me. Yup. Been there, done that, lived the lie. And underneath all that imitation happiness, behind the mask, I was still empty, still broken, still desperate.

Our churches are full of broken people—I'm one of them! And that's OK. God doesn't expect us to be perfect. But Sunday morning comes, and too many of us put on our masks and pretend that everything is just as it should be.

Why are we afraid to show our brokenness? Why can't we see what God sees in us?

There is beauty in brokenness.

There is healing in brokenness.

Because in our brokenness, Jesus shines.

*God began doing a good work in you, and I am sure he
will continue it until it is finished when Jesus Christ
comes again.* (Philippians 1:6)

Getting Real with God

Now, I've talked about how God created each one of us
as a beautiful, unique creation. And I've shared how I believe
he has a plan for us and has given each of us a special destiny.
But when a faulty self-image has you trapped in a prison of
worthlessness, you're not ready to hear those truths. You're
not ready for another well-meaning person telling you how
special you are. You don't want to hear someone else's
notions of divine purpose. As true as it all is, it's just too big
to grasp when you feel completely empty and totally broken.

At the time in my life when I felt that way, I wanted
something much simpler. I just wanted to be OK. I just wanted
to feel real. I wanted to feel like Natalie, the real Natalie, not
like a disgustingly dishonest fake.

For so long I felt like a fake even in my prayers. I
thought they had to be perfect too, full of *thees* and *thous*
and flowery language I would never use if I were being my

real self. It was when I finally realized I could come to God and have a conversation that he became real to me, my real Friend. And as my prayers became real, His Word become life to me. All the scriptures I had head knowledge of as a child were finally taking root in my heart, especially when I found a Bible version that translated and paraphrased the ancient texts into modern-day language that is easier for me to understand and study.

Another step that helped me a lot was to understand that life is full of hard realities *for everyone*. Sooner or later, we all face challenges that have the potential to send us toppling toward the brink of despair. How well I know that no matter how perfect things may look on the outside of your life, you may be dealing with real hurts and hardships that no one else can see. Things happen that we don't, and may never, understand. Those who survive life's difficulties are the ones who recognize the truth: Jesus never promised that life would be easy. But he did promise to be with us even in the most difficult times.

There's a passage in the book of Isaiah that talks about the rough places in our lives. It says, "When you pass through the waters. . . . When you walk through fire . . ." (43:2). Unfortunately it doesn't say "if" or "maybe" but "when"—as in, it *is* going to happen. But that same passage assures us, as do many verses throughout God's Word, that God will be with us in those hard places. He is on our side, and he believes in us.

Jesus was with me every time I knelt on the cold bathroom floor. Forcing myself to vomit wasn't his plan for me. He loves me, and he didn't like it when I did it. It hurt him to see me hurting myself, but he stayed with me. He never lost his patience, he never gave up, and he never stopped loving me.

The Girl Within

Shannon, twenty-four, sits comfortably in a cozy wing chair, the light of the noonday sun streaming in through the window over her shoulder. A mother of two small children, she smiles at the blocks and toys scattered at her feet. "This is the season of my life that I've always looked forward to," she says. "Having a great husband and being a mommy—this was my dream, the subject of many prayers, and the thing I worried about most. I was convinced, for a while, that it would never happen."

"But why would you think such a thing?" is the obvious question to ask this brunette, all-American young woman.

"Because," she answers matter-of-factly, "I just never thought anyone could love me as I was. I was the friend-girl, not the girlfriend. I was the studious, heavyset girl that guys tried desperately to avoid—unless, of course, they wanted to ask about one of my gorgeous female friends. For two years,

I watched my girlfriends date, get engaged, and get married—all without a single speck of interest in me from the opposite sex."

Even before college, Shannon had been a yo-yo dieter, losing fifteen pounds, gaining thirty, losing forty, gaining thirty-five, all the while wondering why her size seemed to be all that mattered to her peers. "The girl within me was smart, kind, and considerate," she said. "She was fun, a great conversationalist. She was a fairly happy person and had plenty of love to share with the right guy, but she couldn't even buy a date, much less develop a relationship. I tell you, it was enough to make a girl bitter."

In college, everything suddenly changed. Shannon became ill with mononucleosis and had to drop out of school for a semester to recover. The virus weakened her in every way, and the extra pounds disappeared. When she returned to college the first semester of her senior year, her friends almost didn't recognize her, but the guys certainly did.

"I hadn't even been on campus a full day when I was asked out on my very first date," she says, half-excitedly but with irony in her voice. "His name was Paul, and he was beautiful in every way."

Four years, a wedding ring, and two kids later, he's still beautiful, she says. "God has been so good to us, but I'd be lying if I said I didn't worry that someday—if, God forbid, I don't lose all the baby weight or if I my rear begins to spread out like those of the other women in my family—Paul might not love me as much."

It's not a constant fear, she says. She can't afford to be too self-absorbed when there is hide-and-seek to play and diapers to change. But through Bible study and mentoring by mature Christian women, Shannon is beginning to see how valuable she is in God's eyes. The heavy girl she sees in the mirror is showing up less and less, and God's image of Shannon is showing up more and more. The truth of God's Word is impacting not only her marriage but even how she eats, exercises, and takes care of her body.

"I pray that God will help me love myself more because I want to teach my girls to see themselves the way God sees them. And I believe and hope he's doing that."

Chosen by Love

When I finally accepted that Jesus loves me just as I am, right where I am, I started accepting myself. His unfailing, unconditional love was gradually but persistently cemented into my heart as I studied and reflected upon his Word.

A love like that changes a person. It knows every horrible little secret, every selfish, unkind word and still says, "I choose you." It magnifies beauty that has long gone unnoticed, like that of an old painting buried in an attic, worthless and forgotten, until the dust is brushed away and the master artist's signature is revealed, validating the painting's true worth.

Love changes your perception of what is real, what is true, what is beautiful, what is possible. In Isaiah 41:9, the God of the universe says he has chosen me and will not cast me away. I am finally accepted. In Isaiah 43:1 he continues to tell me I am his; he says he calls me by name. *He knows my name!* I finally belong. And in Romans 5:8 I am told that Jesus demonstrated his great love for me when he died for me. Now, *that* is real, true, sacrificial love. There can be no doubts; I am totally and completely loved.

I am as my Creator made me and since He is satisfied, so am I.

—Minnie Smith

If God sees me as priceless, as a treasure, as one worthy of sacrificing his only Son for, how can I believe less of myself? To believe myself unlovable, unreachable, or unacceptable is to believe that God made a mistake. And God does not make mistakes.

Psalm 147:5 says that God's "understanding is infinite" (NKJV). Anyone capable of mistakes would be finite, not infinite. God is not like me. I make mistakes and misjudgments. I change my mind and say things I don't mean. I have destructive thoughts at times. Not God. His works are wonderful, and he thinks about me a lot (see Psalm 40:5 NKJV)! In fact, as unimaginable as it might seem, God thinks so much about me, and about you, that his thoughts are too many to number.

I belong.

I am accepted.

I am loved.

I am alive.

To say these words and believe them to be true is absolutely mind-blowing. In the midst of my struggles with self-acceptance, I came to understand that God really knows me—inside and out. He knows when I'm faking, and he knows when I'm being real with him. He desires the real me. And he wants nothing more from me than that.

The Real You

God went to great lengths to make sure that each of us is an original. Each of us has been given a distinct personality, different likes and dislikes, unique senses of style, and even different ways of learning, thinking, speaking, and interacting with others. Some people are extroverted and outgoing; others are more timid and laid back. Some people are all about glamour and makeup and trendy clothes; others are jeans-and-T-shirt people who don't care about fashion trends.

Some people are self-absorbed and judgmental; others are caring and concerned with justice. Some people close their eyes and lift their hands during worship; others worship God in silence and reserved reverence. God *expects* us to be different. He wouldn't have it any other way. After all, he is our Creator, the Author of variety!

In the space below, write a prayer of thanksgiving for the gifts, attributes, and blessings God has bestowed upon you—his irreplaceable you!

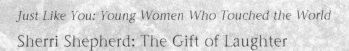

Just Like You: Young Women Who Touched the World
Sherri Shepherd: The Gift of Laughter

Sherri Shepherd is living the American dream. An up-and-coming actress and comedienne, Sherri is making her mark in Hollywood after years of landing guest spots on everything from Friends *to*

Emeril to Everybody Loves Raymond and finally awarded a regular role in the ABC sitcom Less Than Perfect. This year she co-starred with Queen Latifah in the movie Beauty Shop and joined Bernie Mac and Ashton Kutcher in the movie Guess Who.

Being famous had been her dream since the age of four. But life on the way to the dream wasn't paved with glitter. And it certainly wasn't always funny.

Born and raised in Chicago, Sherri knew the sting of racial prejudice, but comedy made the hurt somehow bearable. When she was seventeen, her parents divorced, and her mother relocated Sherri and her three sisters to California. She was a senior in high school in a strange new city. She had no friends. Her mother was gone most of the time, working two jobs. She missed her father. And so as many teenagers do, Sherri rebelled and became sexually active.

She jumped from one unhealthy relationship to another, and then, after one boyfriend went to prison for robbery, Sherri began to consider the direction of her life. Inspired by performances she'd seen and encouraged by friends, Sherri started putting together her own stand-up comedy act. Her routine was as sexually graphic as her life was. Then one day, while riding a city bus, Sherri witnessed a young man helping an elderly woman. Impressed, she introduced herself, and immediately he asked her if she knew Jesus. The year was 1993, and within a matter of months Sherri became a Christian.

But like any new Christian, it took Sherri some time to grow in her faith. An office worker by day and struggling comedienne by night, she didn't clean up her act all at once. Soon, Twentieth Century Fox offered her a fifty-thousand-dollar development deal, and she was torn between trying to honor God with her life and still find comedic success. But God continued to whisper in her ear, urging her to go deeper in her relationship with him. And slowly, Sherri began to give over every aspect of her life and her career to God. "I spent time alone on my knees, praying and crying about the things I needed to repent of. Through it all, God reassured me, I love you despite your faults; because of Jesus, you're pure and whole."

In 1997 Sherri married Jeff Tarpley, a comedian she'd dated before but broke up with because he wasn't a Christian. A year after their breakup, Jeff had accepted Christ, and their relationship was also born again and rock-solid, founded on faith.

Today, Sherri's faith in God is what keeps her grounded, especially in the plastic world of Hollywood. She works hard to make her comedy relevant and yet clean, believing laughter is a healing gift of God. She lets her life do the talking, and she pursues acting with her convictions intact, refusing to curse or do sex scenes. And as God opens doors of opportunity for her, she continues to let the light of Christ shine through her. "I believe God put me on Less Than Perfect," she says, "if for no other reason—to love everyone around me. That's clearly why I'm here."

The Girl Gets Real

Oh, I just want to be me,

And now we come to the epilogue, the place in the book where I write about how my self-worth and sense of value are permanently strong and firmly embedded in my psyche, and how I'm now 100 percent finished with the battle.

But the truth is, I'm still a work in progress. Without my mask on, I admit to you that I'm nowhere near perfect. My struggles continue. I'm human after all, and I see through human eyes. The mirror still screams my imperfections back at me, and I would be dishonest if I said I was never tempted to make my way back to that porcelain throne and kneel to it as my god.

Every day I have choices. I can choose to return to my old ways, to become the old Natalie again and live in bondage to a poor self-image and the ramifications it carries. Or I can choose the life God wants me to have, the freedom Jesus died to give me.

Seems like it would be a very simple choice to make, doesn't it? But the truth is, it's not always easy, given my profession. I'm always in front of people. The pressure for perfection still exists. People are constantly scrutinizing my looks. *I* scrutinize my looks, occasionally fretting because I look my best only when someone else does my hair and makeup. There are still photo shoots to be completed, and many of my photos are still "touched-up." That's when the mind games are most poisonous, when I fight the pressure to be perfect and look like the Natalie Grant on the cover of my latest CD.

Some days I'm stronger than others. To get through the difficult times with my self-worth intact, I recall again and again, throughout the day, the truth of God's Word. The Bible says I am "crowned . . . with glory and honor" (Psalm 8:5 NKJV), that I am more than a conqueror (see Romans 8:37 NIV), and that God even sings over me (see Zephaniah 3:17)! He *chose* to create me. I am the only *me*.

So I'm done trying to be anyone else. I'm a broken

believer, and that's OK because I bring my pieces to the One who can make me whole.

I'm still not perfect, but (even better!) I'm the genuine article now: the real me, the girl God sees.

The Real Me:
WHO GOD SAYS I AM

To help you remember how God sees you, here are some gifts from Scripture to copy and take along wherever you go. Be creative! Decorate some index cards, write out the Scripture passages, then tuck them in your purse, tape them to your mirror, and reread them often to reinforce the truth of God's beautiful creation: *the real you!*

I AM . . .
FORGIVEN

In Christ we are set free by the blood of his death,
and so we have forgiveness of sins.
(Ephesians 1:7)

I Am . . .
Made New in Christ

If anyone belongs to Christ, there is a new creation.
The old things have gone; everything is made new!
(2 Corinthians 5:17)

I Am . . .
Blessed and Chosen by God

In Christ, God has given us every spiritual
blessing in the heavenly world. That is, in Christ,
he chose us before the world was made
so that we would be his holy people. . . . That was
what he wanted and what pleased him.
(Ephesians 1:3–5)

I Am . . .
Strong

Finally, be strong in the Lord and
in his great power.
(Ephesians 6:10)

I Am . . .
HOLY AND WITHOUT BLAME

But be holy in all you do, just as God, the One who
called you, is holy. It is written in the Scriptures:
'You must be holy because I am holy.'"
(1 Peter 1:15–16)

I Am . . .
SET FREE

So Jesus said to the Jews who believed in him,
"If you continue to obey my teaching, you are truly
my followers. Then you will know the truth,
and the truth will make you free."
(John 8: 31–32)

I Am . . .
COMPLETE

You have a full and true life in Christ, who is ruler
over all rulers and powers.
(Colossians 2:10)

I Am . . .
Not Guilty

So now, those who are in Christ Jesus are not judged guilty.
(Romans 8:1)

I Am . . .
At Peace with God

All this is from God. Through Christ, God made peace
between us and himself, and God gave us the work of
telling everyone about the peace we can have with him.
(2 Corinthians 5:18)

I Am . . .
Protected

We know that those who are God's children do not
continue to sin. The Son of God keeps them safe,
and the Evil One cannot touch them.
(1 John 5:18)

I Am . . .
Marked As God's

And in Christ, God put his special mark of ownership on
you by giving you the Holy Spirit that he had promised.
(Ephesians 1:13)

I Am . . .
Created for Good

God has made us what we are. In Christ Jesus, God made
us to do good works, which God planned in advance for
us to live our lives doing.
(Ephesians 2:10)

I Am . . .
Loved

Brothers and sisters, God loves you,
and we know he has chosen you.
(1 Thessalonians 1:4)

I Am . . .
Becoming More Like Christ

Our faces, then, are not covered. We all show the
Lord's glory, and we are being changed to be like him.
(2 Corinthians 3:18)

I Am . . .
Not Afraid

God did not give us a spirit that makes us afraid but
a spirit of power and love and self-control.
(2 Timothy 1:7)

I Am . . .
Never Alone

We have troubles all around us, but we are not defeated.
We do not know what to do, but we do not give
up the hope of living. We are persecuted,
but God does not leave us. We are hurt sometimes,
but we are not destroyed.
(2 Corinthians 4:8–9)

Additional Resources

READING RESOURCES

In my journey toward a better understanding of my struggle with bulimia, as well as my relationship with God and His perspective on my life, I have found the following reading resources insightful and beneficial. I'm confident you'll find them the same for you.

Neil T. Anderson, *The Bondage Breaker: Overcoming Negative Thoughts, Irrational Feelings and Habitual Sins*, 2nd edition (Eugene, OR: Harvest House, 2000).

The title basically says it all. If you're tired of living in a mental or emotional rut, this book could well be the tow truck that pulls you out.

Henry Blackaby and Claude King, *Experiencing God: Doing the Will of God* (Nashville, TN: Broadman & Holman, 1998).

Hundreds of thousands of Christians, myself included, have been propelled by this book to a deeper knowledge of God that comes through intimate love relationship with

Him. If you want to discover how God is at work in your life, this is a great place to start.

Drs. Marlene Boskind-White and William C. White, *Bulimia Anorexia: The Binge-Purge Cycle and Self Starvation* (New York: W.W. Norton, 1987).

This is a basic primer on eating disorders written from a clinical perspective by two therapists who were pioneers in the psychological treatment of bulimia and anorexia. Although it isn't written from a Christian worldview, there is still a lot of great information here, and it's not so clinical that it's unreadable.

John and Stasi Eldredge, *Captivating: Unveiling the Mystery of a Woman's Soul* (Nashville, TN: Thomas Nelson, 2005).

By revealing the core desires every woman shares—to be romanced, to play an irreplaceable role in a grand adventure, and to unveil beauty—John and Stasi Eldredge invite women to recover their feminine heart, created in the image of an intimate and passionate God.

Dr. Gregory L. Jantz, *Hope, Help and Healing for Eating Disorders: A New Approach to Treating Anorexia, Bulimia and Overeating* (Colorado Springs, CO: Shaw, 2002).

Eating disorders affect the whole person, yet treatments often focus on emotional issues alone. In this powerful book, Dr. Jantz fills in the gaps left by traditional treatment programs, tackling not only the emotional but also the all-too-often-ignored relational, physical, and spiritual dimensions of healing.

Joyce Meyer, *Approval Addiction: Overcoming Your Need to Please Everyone* (New York: Warner Faith, 2005).

Joyce Meyer speaks from personal experience about how to overcome insecurities—often stemming from abuse—and how to begin to live for God's approval alone, free from the need to please.

Donald Miller, *Searching for God Knows What* (Nashville, TN: Thomas Nelson, 2004)

In *Searching for God Knows What,* Donald Miller's provocative and funny book of essays, the main theme is humanity's constant search for redemption, and how the inability to find it leads to chaotic relationships, self-hatred, the accumulation of meaningless material possessions, and a lack of inner peace. He doesn't necessarily offer solutions but points out that there is much about the journey that we can learn from.

Beth Moore and Dale McCleskey, *Breaking Free: Making Liberty in Christ a Reality in Life* (Nashville, TN: Broadman & Holman, 2004).

When Beth Moore—one of today's most prolific Christian writers—says she's never written anything that means more to her than this book, you'd better believe it's important. This book can revolutionize your faith. It certainly has mine.

Angela Thomas, *Do You Think I'm Beautiful? The Question Every Woman Asks* (Nashville, TN: Thomas Nelson, 2003).
Angela's book beautifully identifies the longing all women share—the desire to be unconditionally loved, pursued, and seen as beautiful—and how to return to the One who makes those desires reality.

COUNSELING RESOURCES

If you're at a place in your life where you need Christian counseling to help you overcome an eating disorder, you may want to consider the following:

Mercy Ministries exists to transform lives of girls struggling with life-controlling issues by providing free residential care and life skills training through biblical counseling in a loving environment. For more information, visit their Web site at www.mercyministries.com.

Remuda Ranch provides intensive inpatient programs for women and girls suffering from anorexia and bulimia and related issues, offering hope and healing through a biblically based program. For more information, visit their Web site at www.remuda-ranch.com or call 1-800-445-1900.

TurningPoint Counseling, with fifteen locations throughout California, offers Christian counseling for eating disorders. For more information, visit their Web site at www.turningpointcounseling.org or call 1-800-99-TODAY.

To find a state-licensed or certified Christian counselor in your area or to find out about other treatment facilities and organizations that offer help for eating disorders, please visit the **American Association of Christian Counselors** Web site at www.aacc.net.

NOTES

1. Excerpt from *Posers, Fakers, and Wannabes: Unmasking the Real You* by Brennan Manning, ©2003. Used by permission of NavPress. www.navpress.com All rights reserved.

2. Elisabeth Kübler-Ross, M.D. Used by permission. www.elisabethkublerross.com.

3. "God Is In Control," Gary Driskell, ©1994 Word Music, LLC. All Rights Reserved. Used by Permission.

4. Excerpt from *A Big Enough God* by Sara Maitland, ©1995 by Sara Maitland. Reprinted by permission of Henry Holt and Company, LLC.

About the Author

*N*atalie Grant grew up in Seattle in a loving home filled with five children and two parents who gathered each night for family time at the dinner table.

Natalie's musical talent was recognized at an early age, and she began performing when she was just three years old. Her ability continued to develop throughout high school and into college, which she attended on a music scholarship.

In 1999, she recorded her first album, *Natalie Grant.* Since then she has recorded three more, each one showing Natalie developing into more than a singer but also an impassioned songwriter. *Stronger,* Natalie's second album, featured three Top Ten radio hits and gained Natalie her first Dove Award nomination for Female Vocalist of the Year. Her next album, *Deeper Life,* included several songs Natalie had written herself, and it garnered mainstream attention. "No Sign of It," one of the tracks from *Deeper Life,* was featured in the major motion picture *A View from the Top,* starring Gwyneth Paltrow and Mike Meyers and was also one of the Top Fifty–played songs on mainstream radio for 2003.

Her latest album is the best-selling and critically acclaimed *Awaken* on Curb Records, which includes her number-one-hit song, "Held." Other songs on the *Awaken* album feature hauntingly beautiful lyrics that reveal her passion for those trapped in the tragedy of human trafficking.

As an outgrowth of that passion, Natalie has established The Home Foundation, an organization committed to helping children who have been sold into slavery and prostitution in India.

Natalie is now a three-time Dove Award nominee for Female Vocalist of the Year and continues to share her music around the world. She's also a frequent guest artist for the nationwide Women of Faith conferences and for the new Revolve Tour, Women of Faith's nationwide conference for teen girls.

She and her husband, music producer Bernie Herms, make their home in Nashville, Tennessee.

For more information on The Home Foundation and details on how you can help, go to www.nataliegrant.com.